I0307357

Rigor in the K–5 ELA and Social Studies Classroom

Learn how to incorporate rigorous activities into your English language arts or social studies classroom and help students reach higher levels of learning. Expert educators and consultants Barbara R. Blackburn and Melissa Miles offer a practical framework for understanding rigor and provide specialized examples for elementary ELA and social studies teachers. Topics covered include:

- Creating a rigorous environment
- High expectations
- Support and scaffolding
- Demonstration of learning
- Assessing student progress
- Collaborating with colleagues

The book comes with classroom-ready tools, offered in the book and as free eResources on our website at www.routledge.com/9781138598959.

Barbara R. Blackburn, a Top 30 Global Guru in Education, has taught early childhood, elementary, middle, and high school students and has served as an educational consultant for three publishing companies. In addition to speaking at international, national, and state conferences, she also regularly presents workshops for teachers and administrators in elementary, middle, and high schools. She is the author of over 20 books, including the bestseller *Rigor Is Not a Four-Letter Word*.

Melissa Miles, coauthor of *Rigor in the 6–12 ELA and Social Studies Classroom*, is currently back in the classroom teaching middle school language arts after serving as Director of Educational Resources at a school in Charlotte, North Carolina. She has almost 20 years of classroom teaching experience. She is also twice credentialed as a National Board-Certified teacher for young adolescents, works as a SpringBoard Curriculum consultant to College Board, and is a certified member of the site visitation team for the Schools to Watch award.

Also Available from Barbara R. Blackburn

(www.routledge.com/K-12)

Rigor in the 6–12 ELA and Social Studies Classroom: A Teacher Toolkit
with Melissa Miles

Rigor in the K–5 Math and Science Classroom: A Teacher Toolkit
with Abbigail Armstrong

Rigor in the 6–12 Math and Science Classroom: A Teacher Toolkit
with Abbigail Armstrong

Rigor and Differentiation in the Classroom: Tools and Strategies

Rigor in the RTI and MTSS Classroom: Practical Tools and Strategies
with Bradley S. Witzel

Rigor Is Not a Four-Letter Word, 3rd Edition

Rigor and Assessment in the Classroom

Motivating Struggling Learners: 10 Ways to Build Student Success

Rigor in Your Classroom: A Toolkit for Teachers

Rigor for Students with Special Needs
with Bradley Witzel

Rigor Made Easy: Getting Started

Rigor in Your School: A Toolkit for Teachers
Ronald Williamson and Barbara R. Blackburn

Rigor in the K–5 ELA and Social Studies Classroom

A Teacher Toolkit

Barbara R. Blackburn and
Melissa Miles

Routledge
Taylor & Francis Group
NEW YORK AND LONDON

First published 2020
by Routledge
52 Vanderbilt Avenue, New York, NY 10017

and by Routledge
2 Park Square, Milton Park, Abingdon, Oxon, OX14 4RN

Routledge is an imprint of the Taylor & Francis Group, an informa business

Library of Congress Cataloging-in-Publication Data
Names: Blackburn, Barbara R., 1961– author. | Miles, Melissa (Language arts teacher) author.
Title: Rigor in the K-5 ELA and social studies classroom : a teacher toolkit / Barbara R. Blackburn and Melissa Miles.
Description: New York, NY : Routledge, 2020. | Includes bibliographical references.
Identifiers: LCCN 2019035192 (print) | LCCN 2019035193 (ebook) | ISBN 9781138598935 (hardback) | ISBN 9781138598959 (paperback) | ISBN 9780429486005 (ebook)
Subjects: LCSH: English language—Study and teaching (Kindergarten) | English language—Study and teaching (Elementary) | Language arts (Kindergarten) | Language arts (Elementary) | Social studies—Study and teaching (Kindergarten) | Social studies—Study and teaching (Elementary) | Classroom environment. | Motivation in education.
Classification: LCC LB1576 .B4953 2020 (print) | LCC LB1576 (ebook) | DDC 372.6—dc23
LC record available at https://lccn.loc.gov/2019035192
LC ebook record available at https://lccn.loc.gov/2019035193

ISBN: 978-1-138-59893-5 (hbk)
ISBN: 978-1-138-59895-9 (pbk)
ISBN: 978-0-429-48600-5 (ebk)

Typeset in Palatino
by Apex CoVantage, LLC

Visit the eResources: www.routledge.com/9781138598959

Dedication

We dedicate this book to those who love their content areas and teach with a passion to enhance student learning.

I dedicate this book to my former graduate students at Winthrop University. Each of you had talents and insights, which you used to make a difference with your own students every day. – ***Barbara***

I dedicate this book to my mentor, Barbara. You encourage me, motivate me, counsel me, and tell me the brutal truth . . . even when I don't want to hear it. Most importantly, you've believed in me from the start. Thank you for pushing me and making me the teacher and writer I am today! – ***Melissa***

Contents

eResources

As you read this book, you'll notice the eResources icon next to the following tools. The icon indicates that these tools are available as free downloads on our website, www.routledge.com/9781138598959, so you can easily print and distribute them to your students.

Meet the Authors

Barbara R. Blackburn, named a Top 30 Global Guru in Education, has dedicated her life to raising the level of rigor and motivation for professional educators and students alike. What differentiates Barbara's more than twenty books are her easily executable concrete examples based on decades of experience as a teacher, professor, and consultant. Barbara's dedication to education was inspired in her early years by her parents. Her father's doctorate and lifetime career as a professor taught her the importance of professional training. Her mother's career as a school secretary shaped Barbara's appreciation of the effort all staff play in the education of every student. Barbara has taught early childhood, elementary, middle, and high school students and has served as an educational consultant for three publishing companies. She holds a master's degree in school administration and was certified as a teacher and school principal in North Carolina. She received her PhD in Curriculum and Teaching from the University of North Carolina at Greensboro. In 2006, she received the award for Outstanding Junior Professor at Winthrop University. She left her position at the University of North Carolina at Charlotte to write and speak full time.

In addition to speaking at state, national, and international conferences, she also regularly presents workshops for teachers and administrators in elementary, middle, and high schools. Her workshops are lively and engaging and filled with practical information. Her most popular seminars include:

- Rigor Is NOT a Four-Letter Word
- Rigorous Schools and Classrooms: Leading the Way
- Rigorous Assessments
- Differentiating Instruction Without Lessening Rigor in Your Classroom
- Motivation + Engagement + Rigor = Student Success
- Rigor for Students with Special Needs
- Motivating Struggling Students

Barbara can be reached through her website: www.barbarablackburnonline.com.

Melissa Miles, coauthor of *Rigor in the 6–12 ELA and Social Studies Classroom*, is currently back in the classroom teaching middle school language arts after serving as Director of Educational Resources at a K–8 school in Charlotte, North Carolina, where she supervised tutors, coordinated resources for students with special needs, developed curriculum and pacing guides, and was a resource leader for faculty. She has almost 20 years of classroom teaching experience. Melissa holds an undergraduate degree in middle-level education with a concentration in English and also holds a master's degree in middle-level education with a concentration in language arts. She is also twice credentialed as a National Board-Certified teacher for young adolescents, works as a SpringBoard Curriculum consultant to College Board, and is a certified member of the site visitation team for the Schools to Watch award. Melissa served as Dr. Blackburn's editorial and research assistant for *Classroom Motivation from A to Z, Classroom Instruction from A to Z, Literacy from A to Z*, and *Rigor Is Not a Four-Letter Word*. Her workshops are filled with humor, practical content, and a focus on student ownership of learning.

Acknowledgments

As always, my husband, Pete, is my rock and foundation. He inspires me, encourages me when I am struggling and is the joy of my life. My family – my stepson Hunter, my parents Bob and Rose, my sisters Becky and Brenda, and my brothers-in-law Quinn, John, and Anthony – are always supportive of my work. I'm especially grateful to Missy Miles, my coauthor, my former student, my colleague, and my friend. We've talked about this for a long time, and our dream finally came true. Finally, my friends regularly cheer me on, which feeds my soul.

– *Barbara*

First and foremost, thank you to my husband, who has always been extremely supportive of my professional and personal growth; my mom, who has always modeled a hard work ethic and made numerous sacrifices for me to have opportunities; and my daddy, whose innate teaching spirit lives on in me. I'm also very grateful for my own children's amazing elementary teachers who've inspired me in ways they may not even know: Jennifer Rebsamen, Sherry Harris, Beth Brady, Alydn Keefer, Cathy Gerald, Bethany Baker, and Jocelyn Yasinski. Personally, I have to acknowledge my best friend, Jenn, who continues to build me and be "my person." Finally, to Emma, Eian, and Eli, who allow me to write during our summer "break" and share me with middle school students throughout the year.

– *Melissa*

From Barbara and Melissa

To our colleague and friend Abbigail Armstrong, coauthor of the *Rigor in the Math and Science Classroom* books (K–5 and 6–12), for her collaboration and input, which improved our writing.

To Ron Williamson, coauthor of *Rigor in Your School: A Toolkit for Leaders*, thank you for your thoughts and materials for Chapter 7.

To Brad Witzel, coauthor of *Rigor in the RTI and MTSS Classroom*, for his ideas in Chapter 4 related to students with special needs, thank you for your insights.

To Lauren Davis, for exceptional work helping us merge two voices together into a unified narrative.

To Carlee Lingerfelt and Michael Sudduth for their creation of the original skeleton for the "Flesh It Outs" in Chapter 4.

To Andrea Perdue, Tamikia Samuels, Brenda Blasco, Robin Collins, Kym Zamora and Victoria Hunt for the Social Studies adaptation of "Flesh It Out" in Chapter 4.

To Emma Capel, you came through with a flair for the cover!

To Project Manager Autumn Spalding, thanks for making the production process smooth.

Preface

This book springs from feedback we regularly receive during our workshops. Despite a variety of practical suggestions, teachers always want more . . . particularly in their subject areas.

In Chapter 1, we will discuss the data that supports a need for increased rigor in ELA and social studies, the myths related to rigor and the definition for rigor. In Chapter 2, we'll focus on the aspects of your classroom environment that support rigor. Here, you'll find topics such as student motivation, growth mindset, and developing student ownership. Chapters 3 and 5 are companions covering how to increase expectations, and how to demonstrate learning that meets those expectations. You may choose to read those together.

In Chapter 4, we'll emphasize the support and scaffolding needed to aid students so they can be successful with rigorous work. This is a critical aspect of rigor, and one you want to pay particular attention to. Chapter 6 details aspects of both formative and summative assessment, with specific examples and suggestions for strategies. Finally, in Chapter 7, we'll provide recommendations for working together with other teachers to improve learning. If you are participating in a professional learning community (PLC), hopefully you'll find some new ideas to consider. If you are considering beginning a PLC, we provide a good starting point.

Our goal is for you to immediately use what you read in this book. Each chapter is organized into smaller topics. At the end of Chapters 2 through 7, you'll find *Points to Ponder*, which will allow you to reflect on your learning. Finally, you can contact us through Barbara's website, www.barbarablackburnonline.com. We would like to hear from you as you implement the ideas from the book. One of the best parts of writing a book occurs when teachers and students share how they took an idea and made it their own. As you read the chapters, we hope you will find ideas that will enhance your classroom. Enjoy the journey to new learning!

1

Introduction

Rigor has been an area of increasing focus in education. However, when you talk with teachers and leaders, everyone seems to have a different understanding of what rigor means, especially what it looks like in the classroom. In this chapter, we'll look at why rigor is important, the misconceptions related to rigor, and a clear definition of rigor.

The Call for Rigor

In 1983, the National Commission on Excellence in Education released its landmark report *A Nation at Risk*. It painted a clear picture: test scores were declining, lower standards resulted in American schools that were not competitive with schools from other countries, and students were leaving high school ill-prepared for the demands of the workforce. "Our nation is at risk. . . . The educational foundations of our society are presently being eroded by a rising tide of mediocrity that threatens our very future as a nation and a people." More than 30 years later, similar criticisms are leveled at today's schools.

New Calls for Rigor

Since *A Nation at Risk* was released, the call for more rigor has only increased. *The Condition of College and Career Readiness* (2011), a thorough report from the ACT, has reinforced the lack of preparedness by high school graduates for college and for the workforce. In 2010, the Common Core State Standards (www.corestandards.org) were created to increase the level of rigor in schools. Other recently revised state standards similarly reinforced the need. Rigor is at the center of these standards, and much of the push for new standards came from a concern about the lack of rigor in many schools today, as well as the need to prepare students for college and careers.

Despite these efforts, results indicate a further decline in the progress of American students compared to that of other nations. Rankings from the Progress in International Reading Literacy Study were released in December 2017. This assessment is given to fourth graders across the globe every five years. Our country's ranking dropped from fifth in the world in 2011 to thirteenth in 2016, being surpassed by five countries, including one of the lowest socioeconomic countries in the European Union. Similarly, the Program for International Student Assessment (PISA) is an exam administered every three years to 15-year-old students in seventy-two countries. The 2015 results ranked American students twenty-fourth in reading, having made no statistically significant progress since the previous testing in 2012 (www.oecd.org/pisa/). According to the National Assessment of Educational Progress and the NAEP Reading Report Card from 2017 (released in April 2018), only 37% of our fourth graders are at or above a proficiency level in reading, which is very similar to eighth grade, where only 36% of students in public and private schools across the country are performing at a proficient level (www.nationsreportcard).

International/National Reading Results		
Assessment	*Ranking*	*Score Compared to Highest Score*
PISA 2015 (fourth grade)	24 out of 72	497 compared to 535
PIRLS (fourth grade)	15 out of 50	549 compared to 581
NAEP	37% of fourth grade students scored at or above Proficient 36% of eighth grade students scored at or above Proficient	

Sources: www.oecd.org/pisa/; www.nationsreportcard.gov/reading_2017; https://nicspaull.files.wordpress.com/2017/12/p16-pirls-international-results-in-reading.pdf

It has become apparent that American educators must continue to improve the status of our educational system and the performance of our students. Critical, deliberate research and work on redesigning standards has taken place over the course of the last decade. This, in part, has caused a shift in the way standards are designed to include a concerted focus on rigor in each strand and task. In its *Research Foundations: Empirical Foundations for College and Career Readiness* publication (2014), the College Board acknowledges that "students who take more rigorous course work in high school are more likely to be ready for college and career . . . than students who take less rigorous course work." Moreover, their research has shown that this rigorous instruction must allow students to gain deep understanding of well-chosen topics rather than a surface-level knowledge of numerous topics (https://collegereadiness.collegeboard.org/pdf/research-foundations-college-career-readiness.pdf). In response to research, our educational standards have become centered on essentials and contain focus and clarity for teachers and students. Most recently, the development of the College and Career Readiness standards (CCRs) raises our expectations of the skills American students should be able to master in order to thrive in postsecondary education and/or the workforce.

Key Shifts in the Standards

The Office of Vocational and Adult Education (OVAE) wanted to create a stronger link between adult education, postsecondary education and work. To do so, they evaluated the Common Core State Standards, which had been created based on a broad range of research and with wide input from stakeholders. Then they determined which of those essential skills were most relevant for post–high school plans. Finally, they shared the results in *Promoting College and Career Ready Standards in Adult Basic Education*. Let's look at three critical shifts that need to occur in schools in the areas of English/language arts and content literacy across the curriculum.

English/Language Arts and Literacy in History/Social Studies, Science, and Technical Subjects	
Texts Students Read and Questions for Writing and Speaking	
Shift	*Explanation*
Complexity: Regular practice with complex text and its academic language	♦ Complexity of text that students are able to read is the greatest predictor of success in college and careers (ACT, 2006). ♦ Current gap in complexity between secondary texts and college/career texts is roughly four grade levels (Williamson, 2006).
Evidence: Reading, writing, and speaking grounded in evidence from text, both literary and informational	♦ National assessment data and input from college faculty indicate that command of evidence is a key college and career readiness skills. ♦ Focus is on students' ability to read carefully and grasp information, arguments, ideas, and details based on evidence in the text.
Knowledge: Building knowledge through content-rich nonfiction	♦ Informational text makes up the vast majority of required reading in college and the workplace. ♦ Students need to be immersed in information about the world around them if they are to develop the strong general knowledge and vocabulary they need to become successful readers and be prepared for college, career, and life.

These shifts are critical for all students. A teacher Barbara spoke with said, "My students can't even answer the questions. How am I supposed to ask them for evidence?" Requiring students to provide evidence for opinions and responses is a necessary skill that should start at the kindergarten level. It's simple at any age; just ask, "How do you know?" Rather than accepting a surface-level response, challenge your students to "prove it." If your fifth graders claim that Max Kane from *Freak the Mighty* is insecure, ask them what parts of the text led them to believe that. The extra step requires students to think about motives, characterization, author's craft, etc., which involves a much higher-level thought process occurring. Similarly, when asking second graders why they think it is important to protect honeybees, require them to use evidence from the unit the class just completed on pollenation and food production. Again, the last step in their learning process should ask students to go beyond the text and make relevant connections to the larger world.

In the sample standards that follow, notice the shift from identification and knowledge of a concept to a thorough understanding of the implicit information present in a text.

Sample From College Career Readiness Standards in English Language Arts

CCSS.ELA-LITERACY.RL.3.3

Describe characters in a story (e.g., their traits, motivations, or feelings) and explain how their actions contribute to the sequence of events

CCSS.ELA-LITERACY.RL.3.7

Explain how specific aspects of a text's illustrations contribute to what is conveyed by the words in a story (e.g., create mood, emphasize aspects of a character or setting)

Sample from NCTE/IRA Standards for the English Language Arts

1. Students apply knowledge of language structure, language conventions (e.g., spelling and punctuation), media techniques, figurative language, and genre to create, critique, and discuss print and non-print texts.
2. Students conduct research on issues and interests by generating ideas and questions, and by posing problems. They gather, evaluate, and synthesize data from a variety of sources (e.g., print and non-print texts, artifacts, people) to communicate their discoveries in ways that suit their purpose and audience.

College, Career, and Civic Life

Social studies professionals were also concerned about the lack of rigor, so they developed the College, Career, and Civic Life (C3) Framework for Social Studies State Standards. They used five guiding principles to ensure high-quality standards. Once again, you will notice the emphasis on high-level thinking, or rigor.

Guiding Principles

1. Social studies prepares the nation's young people for college, careers, and civic life.
2. Inquiry is at the heart of social studies.
3. Social studies involves interdisciplinary applications and welcomes integration of the arts and humanities.
4. Social studies is composed of deep and enduring understandings, concepts, and skills from the disciplines. Social studies emphasizes skills and practices as preparation for democratic decision making.
5. Social studies education should have direct and explicit connections to the Common Core State Standards for English Language Arts.

These guidelines are integrated into the standards set forth in the various social studies courses. The following are three sample standards from the College, Career, and Civic Life (C3) Framework for Social Studies State Standards for grades K–2 and 3–5.

D2.Geo.3.K-2. Use maps, globes, and other simple geographic models to identify cultural and environmental characteristics of places.

D2.Civ.3.K-2. Explain the need for and purposes of rules in various settings inside and outside of school.

D2.Eco.14.3–5. Explain how trade leads to increasing economic interdependence among nations.

Career Readiness Competencies

Finally, the National Association of Colleges and Employers (2017) has defined career readiness.

> Career readiness is the attainment and demonstration of requisite competencies that broadly prepare college graduates for a successful transition into the workplace.

What are these requisite competencies? They are skills that are general and apply across all content areas and ones that are critical for student success in the workplace.

Career Readiness Competencies

- Critical thinking/problem solving
- Oral/written communications
- Teamwork/collaboration
- Digital technology
- Leadership
- Professionalism/work ethic
- Career management
- Global/intercultural fluency

Source: www.naceweb.org/career-readiness/competencies/career-readiness-defined/

Although these competencies are not necessarily measured on a standardized achievement test, they are important for a student's long-term success. Many are also integral to the learning process, such as a work ethic and use of digital technology.

Myths About Rigor

Now that we have discussed why rigor is important in the ELA and social studies classroom, let's look at misconceptions about the concept. There are nine commonly held beliefs about rigor that are not true *no matter the content area.*

Nine Myths About Rigor

Myth 1: Lots of homework is a sign of rigor.

Myth 2: Rigor means doing more.

Myth 3: Rigor is not for struggling students or those with special needs.

Myth 4: When you increase rigor, student motivation decreases.

Myth 5: Providing support means lessening rigor.

Myth 6: Resources equal rigor.

Myth 7: Standards alone take care of rigor.

Myth 8: Rigor means you have to quit doing everything you do now and start over.

Myth 9: Rigor is just one more thing to do.

Myth 1: Lots of Homework Is a Sign of Rigor

For many people, the best indicator of rigor is the amount of homework required of students. Some teachers pride themselves on the amount of homework expected of their students, and there are parents who judge teachers by homework quantity. Realistically, all homework is not equally useful. Some of it is just busywork, assigned by teachers because principals or parents expect it. For some students, doing more homework in terms of quantity leads to burnout. When that occurs, students are less likely to complete homework and may be discouraged about any learning activity.

Myth 2: Rigor Means Doing More

"Doing more" often means doing more low-level activities, frequently repetitions of things already learned. Such narrow and rigid approaches to learning do not define a rigorous classroom. Students learn in many different ways. Just as instruction must vary to meet the individual needs of students, so must homework. Rigorous and challenging learning experiences will vary with the student. Their design will vary, as will their duration. Ultimately, it is the quality of the assignment that makes a difference in terms of rigor.

Myth 3: Rigor Is Not for Struggling Students or Students With Special Needs

Sometimes we believe our students who are struggling, whether they have special needs, are English learners or are challenged with other issues, simply cannot learn at high levels. At times, they cannot answer even basic questions, so we accept that there is a limit to what they can do. Realistically, all students are capable of rigorous work, as long as they have the right support and scaffolding. For example, Dr. Brad Witzel, a colleague of ours, reminds us:

> Just because a student is labeled learning disabled or at risk, it does not mean he or she is incapable of learning. Students with learning disabilities have average to above-average intelligence. Therefore, ensuring their success in school is a matter of finding the appropriate teaching strategies and motivation tools, all of which we can control as teachers.

Myth 4: When You Increase Rigor, Student Motivation Decreases

Because many students do struggle with challenging work, we assume their motivation will decrease. After all, many students already appear to be unmotivated, so what will happen when the work is harder? The truth is that when we "dumb it down" for students, we lessen motivation. They accurately interpret that easier work means we believe they cannot learn, or they become bored, or both. The result is decreased motivation.

On the other hand, when we provide challenging work, reflect our belief in their success with our words and actions and provide specific support to help them succeed, they will be motivated to work at rigorous levels.

Myth 5: Providing Support Means Lessening Rigor

In America, we believe in rugged individualism. We are to pull ourselves up by our bootstraps and do things on our own. Working in teams or accepting help is often seen as a sign of weakness. Supporting students so that they can learn at high levels is central to the definition of rigor. As teachers design lessons moving students toward more challenging work, they must provide differentiated scaffolding to support them as they learn.

Myth 6: Resources Equal Rigor

Recently, I've heard a common refrain: "If we buy this program or textbook or technology, then we would be rigorous." The right resources can certainly help increase the rigor in your classroom. However, raising the level of rigor for your students is not dependent on the resources you have. Think about the resources you have now. How can you use them more effectively? Do you use a textbook that includes true–false tests? Often they are not rigorous because students can guess the answer. However, add one step for more rigor. Ask students to rewrite all false answers into true statements, and it requires students to demonstrate true understanding. It's not the resources; it's how you use them that makes a difference.

Myth 7: Standards Alone Take Care of Rigor

Standards alone, even if they are rigorous, do not guarantee rigor in the classroom. Most state standards and the Common Core State Standards are designed to increase the level of rigor in classrooms across the nation. However, they were not designed to address instruction. In fact, they provide a framework for what is to be taught and what students are expected to know. If implemented without high levels of questioning or applications, the standards themselves are weakened. Your instructional practices, or how you implement standards, are just as critical as the curriculum.

Myth 8: Rigor Means You Have to Quit Doing Everything You Do Now and Start Over

Although there may be times you need to create a rigorous lesson from scratch, in most cases, you can take what you are doing and make adjustments to increase the rigor. For example, if you are teaching math, instead of asking students to always solve problems, provide examples of problems that are already solved and ask them to identify the errors. Or, if you want students to read and summarize scientific information, also ask them to generate research questions based on the information.

Myth 9: Rigor Is Just One More Thing to Do

Rigor is not another thing to add to your plate. Instead, rigor is increasing the level of expectation in all aspects of what you are already doing. For example, if you are working on differentiating instruction, think about how rigor connects. For your lower tiers, it's important to continue to provide rigorous work, although with more support. Rigor is not separate from other components of your classroom, it is a part of them.

What Is Rigor?

You may have heard some of those myths about rigor. But when we delve into what rigor really means, it is focused on student learning.

> Rigor is creating an environment in which each student is expected to learn at high levels; each student is supported so he or she can learn at high levels; and each student demonstrates learning at high levels. (Blackburn, 2012)

Notice we are looking at the environment you create. The trifold approach to rigor is not limited to the curriculum that students are expected to learn. It is more than a specific lesson or instructional strategy. It is deeper than what a student says or does in response to a lesson. True rigor is the result of weaving together all elements of schooling to raise students to higher levels of learning. We will look at a brief description of each of the core areas in what follows, but we will explore each area in more depth, providing specific activities and strategies in upcoming chapters.

Discussion of Areas of Rigor	
Chapter	*Area of Rigor*
2	Environment
3	Expectations
4	Support
5	Demonstration of learning

Expectations

The first component of rigor is creating an environment in which each student is expected to learn at high levels. Having high expectations starts with the recognition that every student possesses the potential to succeed at his or her individual level. Almost every teacher or leader I talk with says, "We have high expectations for our students." Sometimes that is evidenced by the behaviors in the school; other times, however, faculty actions don't match the words. There are concrete ways to implement and assess rigor in classrooms. As you design lessons that incorporate more rigorous opportunities for learning, you will want to consider the questions that are embedded in the instruction. Higher-level questioning is an integral part of a rigorous classroom. Look for open-ended questions, ones that are at higher levels of critical thinking. It is also important to pay attention to how you respond to student questions. When I visit schools, it is not uncommon to see teachers who ask higher-level questions. But for whatever reason, I then see some of the same teachers accept low-level responses from students. In rigorous classrooms, teachers push students to respond at high levels. They ask extending questions. Extending questions are questions that encourage a student to explain their reasoning and think through ideas. When a student does not know the immediate answer but has sufficient background information to provide a response to the question, the teacher continues to probe and guide the student's thinking rather than move on to the next student. Insist on thinking past the concrete, literal answer. A conversation in an elementary school social studies classroom may sound similar to this:

Teacher: How did Rosa Parks play a part in the Civil Rights Movement?

Student: She sat on the bus and refused to move.

Teacher: Absolutely! But what was significant about where she was sitting?

Student: She was in a seat saved for whites.

Teacher: And why was this wrong, according to this time period in history in the South?

Student: Because the people didn't think African Americans deserved equal rights.

Teacher: Yes! So by refusing to move, Rosa Parks was taking a stand against this belief. How did this help the Civil Rights Movement?

Student: She led to the Montgomery Bus Boycott and people stopped riding the buses until the rules were changed. The bus company lost money and more people began to support the idea that everyone deserved the right to sit anywhere, no matter what color of skin they had.

As you can see, by probing further and expecting more complex responses from students, teachers can assist them in gaining deeper meaning and making more thorough connections. The first answer students give is oftentimes quite concrete and literal, but if you consistently push them to peel back layers and apply higher-level thought processes, they will eventually realize you expect high-level thinking and begin doing it naturally. This will increase the level of rigor in your classroom.

Scaffolding for Support

High expectations are important, but the most rigorous schools assure that each student is supported so he or she can learn at high levels, which is the second part of our definition. It is essential that teachers design lessons that move students to more challenging work while simultaneously providing ongoing scaffolding to support students' learning as they move to those higher levels.

Providing additional scaffolding throughout lessons is one of the most important ways to support your students. Oftentimes students have the ability or knowledge to accomplish a task but are overwhelmed by the complexity of it, therefore getting lost in the process. This can occur in a variety of ways, but it requires that teachers ask themselves during every step of their lessons, "What extra support might my students need?" It is up to the teacher, as practitioner, to anticipate where students may hit roadblocks and to react in the moment in providing additional stair steps for students as needed.

Examples of Scaffolding Strategies

- Asking/using guiding questions
- Preteaching vocabulary
- Chunking the text
- Highlighting or color-coding steps in a project
- Visualizing the text/significant events
- Modeling with think-alouds
- Diffusing difficult vocabulary words
- Marking the text as a way of interacting with and making meaning of it
- Accessing prior knowledge
- Writing standards as questions for students to answer
- Utilizing visuals and graphic organizers such as models for brainstorming and prewriting, maps to accompany history lessons or color-coded paragraphs to help students make meaning of texts
- Employing an "I do—we do—you do" approach as a gradual release of responsibility

If a particular standard requires second grade students to understand how producers and consumers affect the economy, but the student has difficulty accessing the grade-level text, perhaps the teacher can offer a short biographical/documentary video to build background knowledge and then diffuse the difficult vocabulary in the text or provide guiding questions that naturally chunk the text. These scaffolding strategies will allow Student A to reach the same end goal, which is mastery of the standard.

Similarly, if a third grade student struggles with writing, but standards require skills in narrating a story, a teacher might first break down the elements by allowing the student to draw the sequence of events on a storyboard, then tell the story verbally in his or her own words using the picture sequence and finally, attempt to write the story on paper. Afterward, the students may need to read a mentor text and circle the descriptive details that enhance the story, use a graphic prganizer to brainstorm descriptive details to include in his or her own story, and finally add in the details that seem to fit well. These activities would be the "in-between" steps to help the student achieve the standard of being able to use sequencing and descriptive details to tell a story.

Demonstration of Learning

The third component of a rigorous classroom is providing each student with opportunities to demonstrate learning at high levels. There are two aspects of students' demonstration of learning. First, we need to provide rigorous tasks and assignments for students. What we've learned is that if we want students to show they understand what they learned at a high level, we also need to provide opportunities for students to demonstrate they have truly mastered that learning at more than a basic level. Many teachers use Bloom's Taxonomy or Webb's Depth of Knowledge (DOK; Level 3 or above is rigorous). We prefer Webb's DOK for a more accurate view of the depth and complexity of rigor, and we'll explain that more fully in Chapter 3.

Examples of Guidelines for Rigor for Bloom's Taxonomy and Webb's Depth of Knowledge	
Bloom's Taxonomy	*Webb's DOK Level 3*
Analyzing	Does the assessment focus on deeper knowledge?
Evaluating	Are students proposing and evaluating solutions or recognizing and explaining misconceptions?
Creating	
**Please note that although the verbs are important, you must pay attention to what comes after the verb to determine if it is rigorous.	Do students go beyond the text information while demonstrating they understand the text?
	Do students support their ideas with evidence?
	Does the assessment require reasoning, planning, using evidence and a higher level of thinking than the previous two levels (such as a deeper level of inferencing)?

Second, in order for students to demonstrate their learning, they must be engaged in academic tasks, precisely those in the classroom. In too many classrooms, most of the instruction consists of teacher-centered, large-group instruction, perhaps in an interactive lecture or discussion format. The general practice during these lessons is for the teacher to ask a question and then call on a student to respond. While this provides an opportunity for one student to demonstrate understanding, the remaining students don't do so. Another option would be for the teacher to allow all students to think-pair-share, respond with thumbs up or down, write their answers on small whiteboards and share their responses or respond on handheld computers that tally the responses. Such activities hold each student accountable for demonstrating his or her understanding.

Conclusion

The need to increase rigor in our schools is critical if we want to appropriately prepare our students for life after high school, whether that is a postsecondary college, the military or going directly into the workforce. Rigor, however, is more than simply making things harder for students. It is a weaving together of high expectations, scaffolding and support, and demonstration of learning. If we hold our students to high standards and provide them the right support, they will be successful.

2

Creating a Rigorous Environment

One part of rigor that is often overlooked is the classroom environment. However, the culture of a classroom impacts how students work at rigorous levels, if at all. There are five specific areas we can address to create a rigorous environment.

Five Areas

1. Student motivation
2. Growth mindset
3. Building respect
4. Creating safety and security
5. Developing student ownership

Student Motivation

If you've read *Motivating Struggling Leaners: 10 Strategies to Build Student Success*, you know that Barbara believes all students are motivated, just not necessarily by the things we would like. Many of our students are not motivated by a desire to learn; rather, they are motivated by the approval of their friends or the wish to earn some money or something else in their lives. To build a rigorous classroom environment, we need to encourage students' intrinsic motivation so they are not totally dependent on outside rewards.

Students are more motivated when they value what they are doing and when they believe they have a chance for success. Those are the two keys: value and success. Do students see value in your lesson? Do they believe they can be successful?

Value

There are many recommendations relating rigor to relevance. That is the value part of motivation. Students are more motivated to learn when they see the value, or the relevance, of the knowledge and skills presented to them. Students have a streaming radio station playing in their heads: WII-FM—*What's In It for Me*? When we are teaching, students are processing information through that filter. What's in this lesson for me? Why do I need to learn this? Will I ever use this again?

Ideally, your students will make their own connections about the relevance of content, and you should provide them opportunities to make those connections independently. But there are also times that you will need to facilitate that understanding. I observed a fourth grade teacher who was very effective in helping his students see value in lessons. At the beginning of the year, he asked his students to write about their goals for life after high school. Later, when he encountered much apathy from his students during a short unit on poetry, he realized that one particular student was completely tuning him out. He asked her, "Why should poetry be important to you?" Puzzled, she replied, "I don't know. I don't think it is." He then guided her to a realization that, since she wanted to be a songwriter, she would need to know about rhyme and rhythm and using words intentionally. Upon realizing the connection between poetry and song lyrics, her motivation to participate in the lesson increased tremendously.

Real-Life Connections

Writing: Writing is a basic from of communicating with someone (i.e., establish pen pals, letters to a parent or friend, text to a family member, etc.)

Research: When searching for information, you need to learn to question whether your source is trustworthy.

Economics (Inflation): A movie ticket and an ice cream cost more than they did even five years ago.

Literature: It's important to see how different characters handle conflict so that we may learn how our choices lead to consequences.

Democracy: You should understand how your voice can be heard and how everyone should get a say in the way decisions are made.

Kindergarten Social Sciences: As an American citizen, you need to know the importance of American symbols such as the flag, the Pledge of Allegiance, the name or picture of current president, the Statue of Liberty, etc.

Community Workers: You need to know the role certain people play to protect and serve us.

Maps: It's important to know where your neighborhood, city, state, and country are located to understand our place in the world.

Students can also see value in activities and in their relationship with you. When we can provide a hands-on, interactive learning experience, students are more engaged and motivated. Students also find value in their relationships. For example, if you think about your most motivated students, you likely had a good relationship with them. Conversely, with your least motivated students, there was probably not a positive connection. It takes time to build a good relationship with our students, but it is an important part of our role as a teacher.

Ways to Connect With Students

- Smile, even if you don't feel like it.
- Ask them questions about their interests outside of school.
- Have namecards on desks or tables the first day of school so they know you care they are here.
- Incorporate their interests into lessons.
- Attend one of their extracurricular events.
- Incorporate ways to learn about them in your instruction.

Success

Success is the second key to student motivation. Students need to achieve in order to build a sense of confidence, which is the foundation for a willingness to try something else. That in turn begins a cycle that results in higher levels of success, both in academic performance and in college and career readiness. Success leads to success, and the achievements of small goals or tasks are building blocks to larger ones.

In Chapters 3–5, we'll look at ways to increase rigor in your classroom. Each recommended strategy is designed to ensure your students' success. However, Chapter 4 will specifically focus on strategies to support their new learning and to scaffold growth to increased levels for every student.

Fixed Mindset Versus Growth Mindset

There is a difference between a fixed mindset and a growth mindset. As Carol Dweck explains, a fixed mindset assumes that our character, intelligence, and creative ability are static and cannot be changed. A growth mindset, on the other hand, adopts the perspective that our intelligence, creativity, and character can change and grow over time.

These two views have a tremendous impact on teaching and learning. If a teacher believes in a fixed mindset, then he or she is saying there is no potential for growth. If a child is intelligent, they will continue to be so. If a student is struggling, it's because he or she just isn't "smart enough."

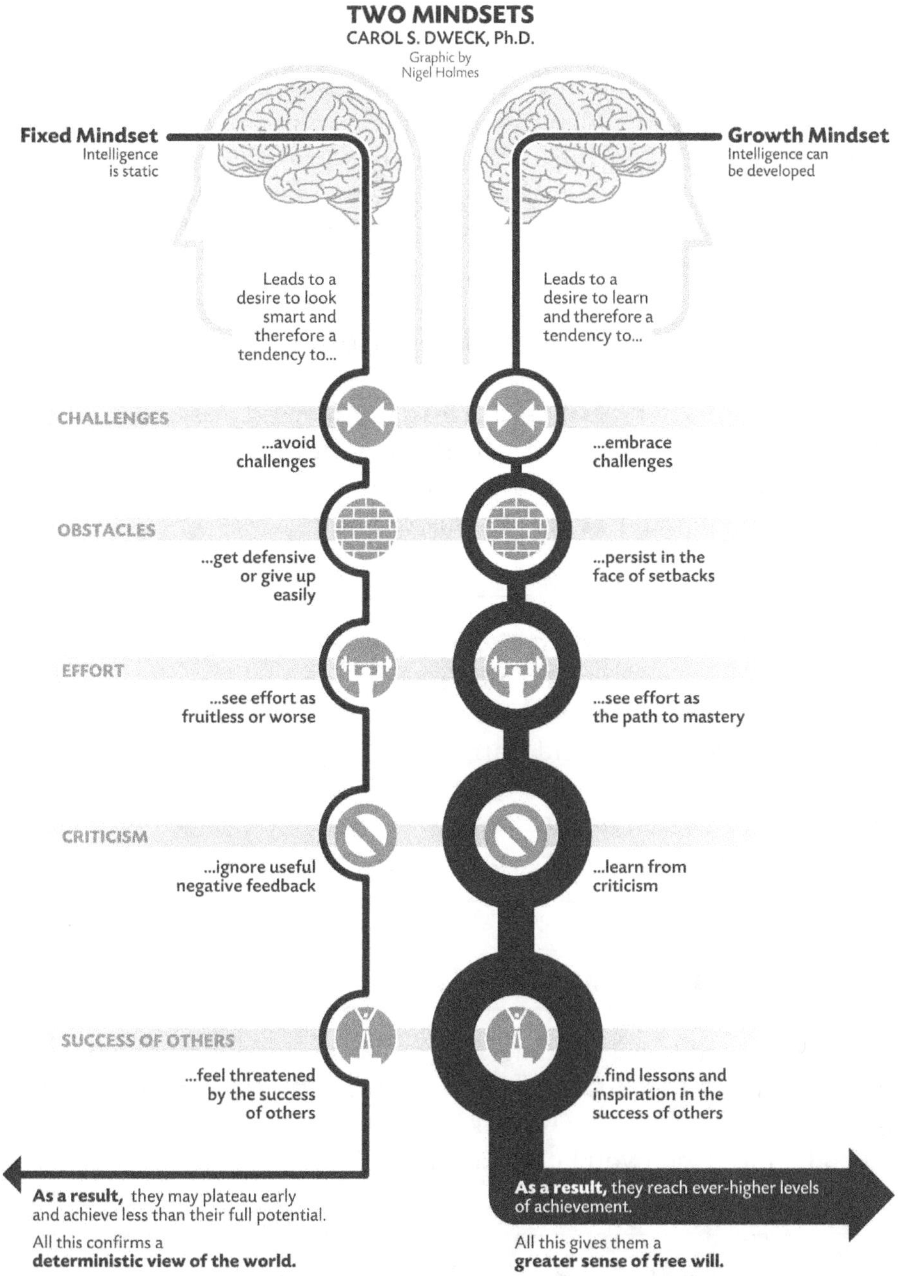

TWO MINDSETS
CAROL S. DWECK, Ph.D.
Graphic by Nigel Holmes
Fixed Mindset
Intelligence is static
Growth Mindset
Intelligence can be developed
Leads to a desire to look smart and therefore a tendency to...
Leads to a desire to learn and therefore a tendency to...
CHALLENGES
...avoid challenges
...embrace challenges
OBSTACLES
...get defensive or give up easily
...persist in the face of setbacks
EFFORT
...see effort as fruitless or worse
...see effort as the path to mastery
CRITICISM
...ignore useful negative feedback
...learn from criticism
SUCCESS OF OTHERS
...feel threatened by the success of others
...find lessons and inspiration in the success of others
As a result, they may plateau early and achieve less than their full potential.
All this confirms a deterministic view of the world.
As a result, they reach ever-higher levels of achievement.
All this gives them a greater sense of free will.

On the other hand, if you believe in a growth mindset, you believe that students may start with a certain amount of ability, but that can change over time with effort and persistence.

For students, which of these they believe also matters. Students with a fixed mindset typically avoid challenges, feel threatened by others' successes, and give up easily. They want to look smart and believe that working hard at a task means they are not smart.

Students with a growth mindset believe they can learn and become better. They embrace challenge, view effort as a positive part of learning, and persist through difficulties. Nigel Holmes provides a clear breakdown of the two mindsets discovered by Dr. Dweck. As you read the table, see if you can identify these traits in your struggling learners.

Strategies to Develop a Growth Mindset in Your Classroom

A growth mindset is critical to a learning-focused classroom. After all, if you don't believe a student can learn and grow, what difference can you make? During the remainder of the chapter, we'll look at six strategies to develop a growth mindset in your classroom.

Strategies to Develop a Growth Mindset in Your Classroom

- Build a learning-oriented mindset.
- Focus on process as well as product.
- Emphasize mastery and learning.
- Reinforce effort.
- Decrease learned helplessness.
- Provide multiple opportunities for success.

Build a Learning-Oriented Mindset

First, we need to ensure that students have a learning-oriented mindset. Often, they don't. Most of our struggling learners had given up, believing they could never learn. As Erika, one of our students, said, "Why are you bothering? Don't you know I'm stupid?"

Sample Fixed-Mindset Student Statements

- I'm never going to be a good writer.
- I'm not good at reading because it takes me forever.
- I don't remember dates well.
- I can't spell.
- This topic has nothing to do with me.
- This assignment is way too difficult for me.

We start the process by having a growth mindset ourselves then constantly and consistently reinforcing it with students. We do this by providing the right support for them to learn, encouraging them along the path and celebrating their resilience and success.

Focus on Process as Well as Product

Another thing we can do to help students develop a growth mindset is to encourage them to focus on the *process* of learning, not just on the *product*. Many of my students just wanted to "get finished." They wanted to do their assignments quickly, and whether they were right didn't matter. After all, they weren't that smart anyway, right?

We need to help students slow down and focus on what they are learning and how they are learning. We recommend a three-step questioning process for students, which can be used for self-assessment.

Questions to Focus on the Learning Process

Before – What do you think you know about Abraham Lincoln?
- What are you unsure about?

During – What questions do you have about Abraham Lincoln?
- What sources might help you find more information about him and this time period in history?

After – Where did you look for help?
- What strategies helped you complete your work?
- How were you successful?

Another time to focus on the process is during classroom discussions. Rather than asking a question, stating whether it is correct or not and moving on, use a roundabout model. For the first round, simply take all possible responses. For the second round, ask students to partner with another student and discuss the responses from the class. They should agree upon the best possible response. In the third round, discuss the partners' picks for the best answer and agree upon an answer. Finally, reflect on the process, with a focus on what helped students decide on the right answer. This takes a bit of time, so you don't need to do it every time you ask a question; just use it periodically.

Focus on Process as Well as Product

Related to the focus on process is the strategy of emphasizing mastery and learning rather than grades. Particularly with older students, there is such a focus on "getting an A" that the joy of learning is lost. Or students are so scared they won't make a good grade that they give up before they start.

Ames and Ames (1990) made an interesting discovery about two school teachers.

> One teacher graded every homework assignment and counted homework as 30 percent of a student's final grade. The second teacher told students to spend a fixed amount of time on their homework (thirty minutes a night) and to bring questions to class about those items they could not complete. This teacher graded homework as satisfactory or unsatisfactory, gave students the opportunity to redo their assignments, and counted homework as 10 percent of their final grade.
>
> Although homework was a smaller part of the course grade, this second teacher was more successful in motivating students to turn in their homework. In the first class, some students gave up rather than risk low evaluations of their abilities. In the second class, students were not risking their self-worth each time they did their homework; rather, they were attempting to learn. Mistakes were viewed as acceptable and something to learn from.

As a result, the researchers recommended deemphasizing grading by eliminating systems of credit points. They pointed out there were positive results from assigning ungraded written work. They also suggested teachers stress the personal satisfaction of doing assignments and help students measure their progress.

Reinforce Effort

Encouraging and reinforcing effort are particularly critical for those students who do not understand the importance of their own efforts. In *Classroom Instruction That Works*, Marzano, Pickering, and Pollock (2001) make two important comments regarding students' views about effort.

Research-Based Generalizations About Effort

- Not all students realize the importance of believing in effort.
- Students can learn to change their beliefs to an emphasis on effort.

(Marzano et al., 2001, p. 50)

This is positive news for teachers. First, we're not imagining it – students don't realize they need to exert effort. And second, we can help them change that belief. Richard Curwin describes seven specific ways to encourage effort.

Seven Ways to Encourage Effort

1. Never fail a student who tries, and never give the highest grades to one who doesn't.
2. Start with the positive.
3. See mistakes as learning opportunities, not failures.
4. Give do overs.
5. Give students the test before you start a unit.
6. Limit your corrections.
7. Do not compare students.

(Curwin, 2010)

Decrease Learned Helplessness

Learned helplessness is a process of conditioning in which students seek help from others even when they have mastered information. See if this example sounds familiar:

A student is asked to draft a topic sentence for an explanatory paragraph, but he immediately raises his hand. When the teacher comes over, the student says he needs help, so the teacher reads the prompt to the student and re-explains the definition of a topic sentence. The student still doesn't answer the question. Next, the teacher provides the student with a sentence frame, but to no avail. Finally, the teacher gives an example of how he might complete the sentence frame by basically writing the sentence for the student.

While this teacher's approach sounds justifiable and maybe even familiar, the teacher is reinforcing the student's learned helplessness. This exchange undermines the student's independent ability to write a topic sentence by himself. Other behaviors that continue a student's learned helplessness include an increased time of completion, lack of academic perseverance, refusal to initiate an attempt and general off-task behavior. Thus, once a student has begun a run of learned helplessness, expect to see the behaviors repeatedly. In this scenario, the student must learn to attend to the teacher's group instruction and attempt to solve problems.

Instead of running to the rescue of students who self-decidely can't succeed without us, or refusing to help such students, it is important to find ways to teach students to gain independence in their problem solving. In other words, find out why the student is behaving in a certain way, and plan a response that best builds academic success and independence. One way to help is to teach students how to learn and succeed without instantly making excuses and asking for help by following these steps.

Steps to Deal With Learned Helplessness

- Determine if learned helplessness exists.
- Explicitly model the preferred academic behavior.
- Teach the student a strategy for displaying the preferred academic behavior.
- Provide practice for the strategy.
- Set a cue to remind the student to initiate the strategy.
- Allow the student to succeed.
- Facilitate the student's problem-solving strategy.

Let's use the following scenario to discuss each step. In a social studies class, students are working to understand a passage on the success of the Jamestown colony. However, Annie hasn't yet begun the assignment. Instead, she repeatedly turns the pages of her picture book and makes grunting sounds of exasperation. The teacher taps Annie's desk as she walks by. Annie rolls her eyes and waves her hand high in a frantic motion like one would make to catch a cab during a rainstorm. The teacher, however, ignores Annie and continues to work with small groups of students. Intermittently, she encourages students who are putting forth effort toward the difficult reading. Annie, irritated that she is being ignored, yells out, "You're not helping me!" (Note: What might look like an insensitive teacher to a passerby is actually a part of an organized effort by school personnel to help Annie overcome learned helplessness. In her IEP [Individualized Education Program], school personnel and Annie's mother agreed to ignore Annie's outbursts when she does not exert effort toward completion of a task.)

A few minutes after Annie's outburst, Annie opens her book and begins to work. The teacher goes over to Annie, leans down, and praises Annie for attempting the assignment. She then reminds Annie that she cannot respond to her when she displays such outbursts, let alone when she does not show effort toward the assignment. The teacher also clarifies with Annie the expectation during independent practice. The teacher spends the next five minutes with Annie going over the passage so that she understands the information.

Provide Multiple Opportunities for Success

We believe strongly that students should have the opportunity to redo work they do not complete at a satisfactory level. Too often, struggling learners do what they consider their best work, yet it is unacceptable. At the primary grades, we talk about mastery learning, the concept that students continue to learn and demonstrate learning until we know they understand. Giving students more than one opportunity to "show what they know" is critical to building a growth mindset, as well as feelings of success.

Ways for Elementary Students to Redo/Reflect on Their Work

Allow a student to record answers or verbally discuss instead of writing them

Allow a student to rework any incorrect items on a test

Allow a student to collaborate with a partner to rework a task, and then do a similar task on his or her own

Allow a student to illustrate or draw rather than write

Allow opportunities for verbal or written student reflection (i.e., "Next time I complete a task like this, I will . . ." or "I am proud of the way I _______ on this task")

Building Respect

A mentor once told us, "Rules without relationship equals rebellion." This couldn't be more accurate when working with teenagers. If you want your middle and high schoolers to invest in your content area and place importance on completing your assignments to the best of their ability, you must first establish a strong rapport with them. The next three sections will focus on building classroom norms to begin this process. Let's start with respect. In order to create a rigorous environment, students must feel that there is a mutual respect between teacher and pupil. Everyone wants to feel as if they are treated fairly and equally. This is no different for your students, whether they are in kindergarten or eleventh grade. In order to establish an atmosphere in which respect reigns, consider asking the students to help you build classroom norms – an agreed-upon set of expectations for conduct in the classroom. Ask students how they want to feel when they are in your room. As they brainstorm a list of words, write them down. Afterward, ask them what they can do to ensure that each classmate experiences these feelings while in the room and write down what you will agree to do as the teacher as well. This is a good starting place for a class contract.

Sample Contract		
When in this class, I want to feel...	*As a member of our community, I can ________ in order to make this happen.*	*As a teacher, I will ________ in order to make this happen.*
♦ safe ♦ liked ♦ involved ♦ smart ♦ productive	♦ encourage my classmates ♦ compliment others' answers ♦ pay attention ♦ avoid laughing at an answer ♦ try my best	♦ not tolerate teasing ♦ welcome your opinions ♦ prepare high-interest, engaging activities ♦ celebrate your successes ♦ provide clear objectives

This student-centered and student-created set of "rules" is more like an evolving, breathing set of guidelines that give life to the learning community in your room. Shared values and a shared vision will allow your students to grow together, make mistakes together, and celebrate achievements together in a mutually respectful atmosphere, where everyone is making the choice to be a part of something greater.

Respect

Relationships are crucial.

Establish an environment of encouragement.

Share your vision.

Provide constructive feedback.

Everyone contributes.

Choice is valued and honored.

Trust is built.

Creating Safety and Security

Maslow's hierarchy of needs teaches us that kids need to feel safe and secure before their mental energy is receptive to academic learning. Not only do our students need to see that we respect them, they need to know that they can trust us. Creating an atmosphere that is full of grace and patience is part of the growth mindset, but it is also critically necessary in leading students to persevere through rigorous material and activities. As educators, part of our job is to invest in the lives of our students by believing in them and pushing them just beyond their perceived limits. Let's look at three strategies for creating an environment that is safe and secure.

Three Strategies

1. Provide risk-free opportunities to learn
2. Encourage students to take risks
3. Teach students to learn from mistakes

Provide Risk-Free Opportunities

The fear of failure paralyzes some of your students. It prevents them from even beginning to attempt your assignment. For many students, it is suffocating to always be under the scrutiny of the red pen, in an environment in which every mistake will be caught and marked and shown no mercy. Where are the opportunities for students to just take a risk and think outside of the box? Do those exist in your classroom? Consider some ways in which you can provide relief for your students and let them explore what works versus what doesn't work without a fear of losing points for trying something new. For example, quickwrites in the ELA or social studies classroom can offer a way for students to put thoughts on paper without being penalized for mechanics and conventions. It is not always necessary to spell every word correctly or have every comma in place, which stifles the thinking process as well as creativity in many reluctant writers. Free up their mental energy to focus on capturing thoughts by giving them a prompt or question and allowing 3–5 minutes for them to JUST write with no grade attached. K–2 students may use drawings and pictures to accomplish this. You may also consider allowing students to provide answers anonymously. You can ask a question at the beginning of class and have students record their response on a sticky note or index card and bring them to you with no name or post them in a designated spot on the board. Students will feel safe in providing their thoughts without fear of being wrong and embarrassed. We'll provide more information on this in Chapter 6, Assessment.

Encourage Students to Take Risks

When students approach a rigorous task, they are taking a risk. Whenever they answer a question, whether in writing or verbally, their knowledge (or lack of) is made visible to those around them. Most students, including your gifted students, do not typically seek out rigorous tasks. They want to complete minimal work, typically to earn a particular grade. If they attempt more than the minimum, working at a level of rigor, it means they are stepping outside their comfort zone. They may or may not be successful, but it is always a learning experience. The first thing you can do to encourage risk taking is to model it for your students. Tell them when you are trying something for the first time and explain that you are nervous. Describe situations in which you have been uncomfortable and share how you adjusted. In both situations, openly reflect about stumbling blocks you experience, including the lessons you learned.

Second, you can provide other models of people who have taken a risk but have succeeded after overcoming obstacles. Ideally, you choose individuals who are specific to your subject area.

Two People Who Have Overcome Failure

Walt Disney

As a young man, Walt Disney was fired from the *Kansas City Star* newspaper because his boss thought he lacked creativity. He went on to form an animation company called Laugh-O-Gram Films in 1921. Using his natural salesmanship abilities, Disney was able to raise $15,000 for the company ($181,000 in 2008 dollars). However, he made a deal with a New York distributor, and when the distributor went out of business, Disney was forced to shut Laugh-O-Gram down. He could barely pay his rent and even resorted to eating dog food.

As if that wasn't enough, Disney also struggled to release some of his now-classic films. He was told Mickey Mouse would fail because the mouse would "terrify women." Distributors rejected *The Three Little Pigs*, saying it needed more characters. *Pinocchio* was shut down during production and Disney had to rewrite the entire storyline. Other films, like *Bambi*, *Pollyanna*, and *Fantasia*, were misunderstood by audiences at the time of their release, only to become favorites later on.

J.K. Rowling

J.K. Rowling, author of the *Harry Potter* books, is currently the second-richest female entertainer on the planet, behind Oprah Winfrey. However, when Rowling wrote the first *Harry Potter* book in 1995, twelve different publishers rejected it. Even Bloomsbury, the small publishing house that finally purchased Rowling's manuscript, told the author to "get a day job."

At the time when Rowling was writing the original *Harry Potter* book, her life was a self-described mess. She was going through a divorce and living in a tiny flat with her daughter. Rowling was surviving on government subsidies, and her mother had just passed away from multiple sclerosis. J.K. turned these negatives into a positive by devoting most of her free time to the *Harry Potter* series. She also drew from her bad personal experiences when writing. The result is a brand name currently worth nearly $15 billion.

Source: Excerpt from: www.growthink.com/content/7-entrepreneurs-whose-perseverance-will-inspire-you

Third, recognize and reward students who are willing to take a chance at something new. This can apply to students who simply exert effort to try a new skill or who are willing to do something new, such as lead a small group or share with the entire class a problem they have solved. You might praise them verbally or use reward certificates.

Sample Certificates

Paws for Progress

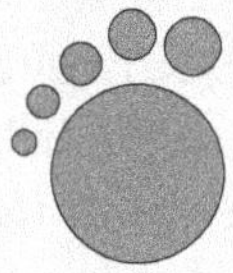

_______________ showed progress

by_____________________________

____

Signed____________

Praise for a Peak Experience

___________________ excelled at

____

____

Signed____________

Lighting Up with Effort

_________________ put forth effort

toward_________________________

____

Signed____________

Owning and Overcoming Mistakes

No matter what you do or what they do to prepare, students will make mistakes. It's part of the learning process. We've learned this as adults, but it is important to continuously emphasize this with students. We've used huge erasers in our classrooms that say, "For really BIG mistakes."

It's laughable, but it gets the point across. Stress to your students that if everything is easy and they never make a mistake, chances are high that they aren't learning or growing. Much more can be learned about individual strengths and weaknesses through failure. As with encouraging risk taking, emphasize to students that acknowledging that you've made a mistake and reflecting on what you learned is an important part of the growth process.

One specific opportunity you can provide to students is to allow them to revisit their formal assessments. When we grade students' work, penalize them for errors and hand the paper back for it to be filed or thrown away, students typically do not learn from their mistakes. One way to change this practice so that it fosters student metacognition is to use a reflective tool after students have taken a test. Kendra Alston shares a sample, which follows. In it, fourth and fifth grade students are provided an opportunity to redo their mistakes, but they are also required to identify what caused the mistake.

Mini-Assessment: Reworking Tests

Name ____

Date of Test ____

Test Title ____

Summarize: What was this passage about?

Identify what you missed and why.
Make a list of what you missed. Place the number that fits beside each item.

1. I didn't understand the question.
2. I thought I had this right.
3. I studied this but forgot.
4. I have no clue about this.
5. I ran out of time and didn't try this.
6. I made a careless mistake.

Question I missed	I chose	Why	Correct answer

You may decide to create a separate grade in your gradebook for assessment revisions. If you want the original test/project grade to remain, require students to make corrections to the graded assessment and give them a quiz grade to represent their capability to address weaknesses and grow from them. Students need time to revisit mistakes in order to overcome them and prevent them from occurring repetitively. This is the essence of rigorous expectations.

Developing Student Ownership

Student ownership is the level in which your students are invested in their own learning. How does ownership increase rigor? When we shift responsibility for learning to students, students take control of their learning, thereby raising the level of content. Do your students have a personal stake in your classroom? If your teaching were a form of government, would it resemble a monarchy, dictatorship or democracy? In order to raise the level of rigor, you'll want to create a democratic environment. This doesn't mean you don't make decisions; rather, you make decisions that build ownership by students. In terms of physical environment, it is better to rearrange straight rows to configure your desks or tables in a manner that promotes and stimulates collaboration. Since your role in a rigorous classroom includes being a facilitator of learning, it's important to allow students to be face to face to make decisions and learn as a group. Create a physical space that encourages interdependence on one another as a community of learners and safe place in which students feel as if they have opportunities for the three components of student ownership: choice, voice, and leadership.

Choice

Students appreciate the opportunity to make choices. No matter the content area, you can integrate "pause points" in your plans at which students get to choose how or when or what they learn. The options for choice may revolve around adjusting your expectations, the content, support and scaffolding, your instruction or demonstration of learning, or assessment, as long as the learning objective remains intact and each task is equally rigorous. Obviously, students do not need choice all the time, but when used purposefully, they appreciate the opportunity to make decisions on behalf of their own learning. You may give them choices in one or all of the areas described in what follows.

Choice Options		
Fifth Grade Biography Research Project		
Support and Scaffolding	*Demonstration of Learning*	*Expectations*
Students may choose to. . .	Students may choose to. . .	Students may choose. . .
♦ watch a short video documentary or biography before reading a text if you lack background knowledge ♦ listen to excerpts of a speech delivered by your subject ♦ use credible online sources ♦ take notes online, on index cards, via voice dictation or using a graphic organizer	♦ present knowledge gained via essay, graphic art, Prezi, photo journal, or monologue	♦ the research topic within certain parameters ♦ the book to read to gather foundational knowledge

Choice Options		
Second Grade Unit on Cultures		
Support and Scaffolding	*Demonstration of Learning*	*Expectations*
Students may choose to. . .	Students may choose to. . .	Students may choose. . .
♦ watch Discovery Ed video clips about various cultures around the world ♦ locate and use picture books about different cultures or written about characters from different cultures ♦ interview people from different cultures ♦ take notes online, on index cards, via voice dictation, or using a graphic organizer	♦ present knowledge gained via poster presentation with pictures and visuals representing the knowledge gained on cultures researched, foldable brochure representing three different clutures, or dress in authentic clothing of a culture studied and teach classmates about it	♦ the culture(s) to study ♦ the picture book to read to gather foundational knowledge

Voice

Students also want to feel that their voice matters, that you hear them, and that you care what they have to say. This is not something that can be faked, as children are true experts in recognizing a lack of sincerity. Ask their opinion. Seek their feedback. Show them that you'll listen. When choosing a picture book biograpy to read in class, let them vote on the title you'll read aloud. This can also be used with homework in the upper elementary grades. For example, you might decide to only give homework three nights a week. If students do not want homework on Thursday nights because most of their other teachers give tests on Fridays, you can probably adjust to that decision. You do not need to do this all the time, but if you provide opportunities for them to participate in decision making, it helps build ownership.

Finally, allow students to share their voice by asking students to help you design the learning. An excellent tool for this is an adaptation of the KWL model, the KWHL.

KWHL			
K *What Do I Know?*	*W* *What Do I Want to Learn?*	*H* *How Can We Learn It?*	*L* *What Did I Learn?*

Notice the opportunities for ownership. Noting what they want to learn helps, but more importantly, this graphic organizer allows students to identify ways the learning can occur. We observed one teacher who used the process as an introduction to a unit on the dinosaurs. The students generated ideas such as going to museum, see if they could find posters and videos online, and search the library to find books about dinosaurs. Their ideas helped students become vested in the learning process.

Leadership

There are a variety of ways you can shift the ownership of learning to the students by allowing them to take the lead. First, you will need to shift your role from director of learning to facilitator. You've likely heard the phrase, "Shift from sage on the stage to guide on the side." That's what this entails. It's a change, and one that requires you to release a bit of control and trust your students. You may think, "My students can't handle it" or "They will get out of control." First, you are still facilitating learning and are very involved in the learning process, just in a different way. Unless students are given opportunities to own their learning, they will never be successful in the process. Here are a few examples of how you can release the onus of learning onto your students.

Leadership Options

Expert Groups: Rather than presenting all of the information on a topic yourself, split it into subtopics and assign small groups the task of becoming experts on their assigned strand. They will be the teachers for that part of the lesson. In the K–2 classroom, each expert group could watch videos and listen to picture books on their topic in order to share information with their peers.

Learning Roles: In cooperative groups, assign a role to each student. As they engage with the learning material (text, video, online presentation, research, etc.), they will each focus on gleaning information from the perspective of their role and come together at the end to share their learning with one another. This places complete ownership on the students. In the K–2 classroom, students could be assigned a character in a picture book, and asked to think about how their character might feel during different points in the book and to decide whather or not that character was making wise decisions.

Reviews: Allow students to generate questions that review the content. You may need to use question stems to help them get started. Then they can rotate asking the questions to each other in small groups. Finally, they can turn these in to you for review and possible inclusion in your assessment. In the K–2 classroom, this might be best facilitated in small teacher-led groups.

Conclusion

It is important that we address the environmental or cultural aspects of our classrooms so that we provide the best opportunity for students to learn at rigorous levels. Student motivation, growth mindset, a respectful attitude, a feeling of safety and security, and a sense of student ownership are the environmental elements that can ensure student success.

Points to Ponder

- The most important thing learned. . .
- One strategy I want to implement now. . .
- One strategy I want to save for later. . .
- I'd like to learn more about. . .
- I'd like to share with other teachers. . .

3

Expectations

In a rigorous classroom, our expectations set the stage for the learning experience. If we communicate lowered expectancies, students will be reluctant to attempt to learn at higher levels. In this chapter, we'll look at five aspects of high expectations.

Five Aspects

1. Behaviors that reflect high expectations
2. Ensuring rigor in your instructional expectations
3. Deeper levels of thinking
4. Projects and project- and problem-based learning (PBL)
5. Passion-based learning: Genius Hour

Behaviors That Reflect High Expectations

Teachers' beliefs, reflected in actions, demonstrate their expectations for their students. In other words, teachers treat students differently dependent on "expectancy," or what they expect. Although the difference in treatment may not be intentional, students notice it and will meet those expectations no matter how high or low they are (Williamson, 2012).

How do our behaviors reflect our expectations? For example, teachers tend to probe students more if they have high expectations. This sends a clear message that "I know you know the answer, and if I give you hints, you will formulate a reasonable response." Teachers also demonstrate expectations in the types of assignments or activities implemented in the classroom. Melissa remembers a time when her gifted students participated in thought-provoking activities such as Socratic seminars, whereas her "general classes" were given texts with questions to answer and had very little opportunity to share their various perspectives.Let's look at typical behaviors related to low and high expectations of students, as described by Robert Marzano (2010).

Differential Treatment of High- and Low-Expectancy Students		
	Affective Tone	*Academic Content Interactions*
Negative	Less eye contact Smile less Less physical contact More distance from student's seat Engage in less playful or light dialogue Use of comfort talk ("That's okay, you can be good at other things") Display angry disposition	Call on less often Provide less wait time Ask less challenging questions Ask less specific questions Delve into answers less deeply Reward them for less rigorous responses Provide answers for students Use simpler modes of presentation and evaluation Do not insist that homework be turned in on time Use comments such as, "Wow, I'm surprised you answered correctly" Use less praise
Positive	More eye contact Smile more More physical contact Less distance from student's seat Engage in more playful or light dialogue Little use of comfort talk ("That's okay, you can be good at other things")	Call on more often Provide more wait time Ask more challenging questions Ask more specific questions Delve into answers more deeply Reward them for more rigorous responses Use more complex modes of presentation and evaluation Insist that homework be turned in on time Use more praise

Marzano also provides a four-step process for identifying and addressing these differences in expectations. We've added suggestions for each step, which are helpful as you consider how to ensure overall high expectations for your students.

Marzano's Four-Step Process to Identifying Expectation Behaviors

Step 1: Identify students for whom you have low expectations.

Create a three-column chart and label the columns High Expectations, Low Expectations, No Expectations. This may be a difficult task, so think of it in terms of assignment completion: Who will turn it in early, who will turn it in on the due date with minutes to spare, and who will not even bother?

Step 2: Identify similarities in students.

Consider ways your students are similar. Ask yourself, "Do I have similar expectations because of my students' similarities?" "Are my expectations high or low?" The similarities may be skin color, ethnicity, cultural group, sex, or gender. This, too, is not an easy task. Discovering our own biases is challenging, but if you confront why you may be treating your students differently, you can begin your journey to equity in expectations.

Step 3: Identify differential of low-expectancy and high-expectancy students (see chart).

Step 4: Treat low-expectancy and high-expectancy students the same.

Choose three behaviors that you discovered you use with students for whom you have high expectations and practice these behaviors for a few days. It may be that you choose to smile at all students. It may be that if any student gives you an incorrect answer, you will give the student process time or time to ask a friend before moving on. Whatever the behavior, keep a log of the behavior and who received the treatment.

Ensuring Rigor in Your Instructional Expectations

In addition to general behaviors related to rigorous expectations, we need to ensure that our instruction is rigorous. Let's look at two common tools teachers use to determine instructional rigor.

Bloom's Taxonomy

Probably the most popular tool used to determine the level of rigor is Bloom's Taxonomy.

> ***Levels of Bloom's Taxonomy***
> Remember
> Understand
> Apply
> Analyze
> Evaluate
> Create

We think Bloom's is a good starting point, but we also find a challenge with this approach. We have come to associate Bloom's levels with specific verbs. However, verbs can be misleading. For example, on the taxonomy, create is at the highest level. But is that always true? When conducting walkthroughs in a school, we observed a lesson in which students were creating get-well cards for a sick classmate. Is that rigorous? Of course not. The verb is deceptive.

Let's look at examples in English/language arts and social studies.

> ***English/Language Arts***
> Analyze the reasons Shirin feels out of place when her family relocates from Tehran to London in the picture book *The Beauty of Difference*.

In this assignment, although students are asked to analyze their responses, they are really just explaining the reasons given in the text. In other words, students are asked to demonstrate understanding rather than provide an analysis.

> ***Social Studies***
> Using all of the materials on your table (gum drops, jelly beans, pipe cleaners, icing, paper, sticky notes, glitter glue, markers), create a map of North America.

In this example, students are asked to create, which is at the highest level of Bloom's Taxonomy. However, when you examine the full assignment, students are simply remembering basic information. Students are asked to design a way to present their information, which may be considered creative, but that doesn't mean the assignment is academically challenging. We believe teachers should provide opportunities for students to demonstrate their creative side, but they should also be rigorous.

Webb's Depth of Knowledge (DOK)

We prefer using Webb's Depth of Knowledge as a benchmark of rigor. Webb's DOK has four levels, focusing on depth and complexity.

Webb's Depth of Knowledge

Level 1: Recall

Level 2: Skill/Concept

Level 3: Strategic Thinking

Level 4: Extended Thinking

As a side note, there is a very popular diagram of DOK on the internet. It is a circle divided into quarters, and each section lists verbs for the level. Simplifying the DOK to verbs takes us back to the same problem as with Bloom's. Verbs can be deceptive.

When writing *Rigor in Your Classroom: A Toolkit for Teachers*, Barbara contacted Dr. Webb's office to ask to reprint the wheel in her book. She received a quick and clear response. Dr. Webb did not create the DOK verb wheel, he does not endorse it, nor does he believe it represents the four dimensions. We understand why. The Depth of Knowledge levels are descriptors of depth and complexity that go far beyond simplistic verbs. Instead, let's look at a detailed description of the DOK levels for English/language arts and social studies.

WebbAlign®

WCEPS
WISCONSIN CENTER for EDUCATION PRODUCTS & SERVICES

SUBJECT	SUMMARY DEFINITIONS OF DEPTH OF KNOWLEDGE (DOK)			
	LEVEL 1	LEVEL 2	LEVEL 3	LEVEL 4
English Language Arts	Requires students to recall, observe, question, or represent facts, simple skills, or abilities. Requires only surface understanding of text, often verbatim recall. ***Examples:*** • Support ideas by reference to verbatim (or only slightly paraphrased) details in text • Use a dictionary to find meanings of words • in a passage • Identify correct spelling or meaning of words	Requires processing beyond recall and observation. Requires both comprehension and subsequent processing of text or portions of text. Involves ordering, classifying text as well as identifying patterns, relationships, and main points. ***Examples:*** • Use context to identify unfamiliar words • Predict a logical outcome • Identify and summarize main points • Apply knowledge of conventions of standard American English • Compose accurate summaries of the major events in a narrative	Requires students to go beyond text. Requires students to explain, generalize, and connect ideas. Involves deep inferencing, prediction, elaboration, and summary. Requires students to support positions using prior knowledge and evidence and to manipulate themes across passages. ***Examples:*** • Determine effect of author's purpose on text elements • Summarize information from multiple sources • Critically analyze literature • Compose focused, organized, coherent, purposeful prose • Evaluate the internal logic or credibility of a message	Requires complexity at least at the level of DOK 3 but also an extended time to complete the task, such as conducting a research project over many weeks. A project that requires extended time but repetitive or lower-DOK tasks is not at Level 4. May require generating hypotheses and performing complex analyses and connections among texts. ***Examples:*** • Analyze and synthesize information from multiple sources • Examine and explain alternative perspectives across sources • Describe and illustrate common themes across a variety of texts • Create compositions that synthesize, analyze, and evaluate

Revised 2014

WebbAlign®

WCEPS
WISCONSIN CENTER for EDUCATION PRODUCTS & SERVICES

SUBJECT	SUMMARY DEFINITIONS OF DEPTH OF KNOWLEDGE (DOK)			
	LEVEL 1	LEVEL 2	LEVEL 3	LEVEL 4
Social Studies	Requires students to recall facts (who, what, when, and where), terms, concepts, trends, generalizations, and theories. May require students to recognize or **identify specific information** contained in maps, charts, tables, graphs, drawings, or other graphics. ***Examples:*** • Recall or recognize an event, map, or document • Describe the features of a place or people • **Identify key figures** in a particular context	Requires students to compare or contrast people, places, events, and concepts; give examples, classify or sort items into meaningful categories; describe, interpret or explain issues and problems, patterns, **reasons, causes, effects, significance or impact,** relationships, and points of view or processes. ***Examples:*** • **Describe the causes/effects** of particular events • Identify patterns in events or behavior • **Categorize events or figures** into meaningful groupings • Convert information from one form into another • Explain issues or problems in their own words	Requires students to draw conclusions, cite evidence, apply concepts to new situations; use concepts to solve problems, analyze similarities and **differences in issues and** problems; propose and evaluate solutions; recognize and explain misconceptions; make connections and explain main concepts. Requires students to justify their arguments through application and evidence. ***Examples:*** • Analyze how changes have **affected people or places** • Apply concepts in other contexts • Form alternate conclusions • Propose and evaluate solutions to problems • Recognize misconceptions and explain them (in their own words) • Make connections across time and place to explain a concept or big idea	Requires complexity at least at the level of DOK 3 but also.an extended time to complete the task. A project that requires extended time but repetitive or lower-DOK tasks is not at Level 4. May require students to connect and relate ideas and concepts within and among content areas. May involve analyzing and synthesizing information from multiple sources; examining and explaining alternative perspectives across a variety of sources; making predictions with evidence as support; planning and developing solutions to problems. ***Examples:*** • Given a situation/problem research, **define and describe the situation/** problem and provide alternative solutions • **Describe, define and illustrate** common social, historical, or geographical themes and how they interrelate

Do you see the deeper structure? It's more comprehensive, which provides a stronger gauge of the rigor of an assignment. Notice that although levels one and two are important, levels three and four are considered rigorous.

Moving to Deeper Levels of Thinking

Let's take a look at examples of tasks and assignments that promote deeper levels of thinking – a critical aspect of rigor. Although we will use Webb's Depth of Knowledge (Level 3) as our base, we will also incorporate facets of rigor from other models, such as the Cognitive Rigor Matrix. First, we'll turn our attention to ELA, then social studies.

Examples

Example One: Research and Writing in English/Language Arts or Social Studies

Choose a historical figure you are interested in learning more about. Create questions to guide your research and a plan for finding information to answer your questions. Use two or three sources to gather information about him or her (one of these can be video). Based on the information learned, determine the most important details you've discovered and categorize/organize them in a graphic organizer. Decide how you would like to share this information with your classmates in a small group, and in your presentation, include how your figure might respond to a particular problem/issue in our society today.

There are several characteristics of a rigorous assignment reflected in example one. Students must synthesize information from numerous sources and determine the most important details to share. They move into level three thinking by considering how their historical figure would react to a particular current-day event.

Example Two: Close Reading Research and Writing with K–1

After reading our book about ants, let's read "The Queen Ant's Birthday" and look for evidence of the different types of ant characters. Who are the worker bees and guard bees, and what do they do for Queen Ant? How does the queen function like the queen bee in our nonfiction book? How do these bees live in community? What can we learn about living in community with one another from these two texts? In addition to using evidence from the texts, provide real-life examples to support your responses.

*Idea adapted from ReadingA-Z.com

In this example, two accessible texts are being paired, requiring a more complex level of analysis and evaluation. Not only do students need to acquire information in the first piece, they must also establish connections between the two different genres and make extended connections to how the same societal roles play out on our communities. This type of assignment could easily apply to any social studies reading as well.

Example Three: Exploring Perspectives One
Dinner Parties

Imagine a dinner party with esteemed guests such as Benjamin Franklin, Thomas Edison, Marie Curie, George Washington Carver, the Wright brothers, and Alexander Graham Bell. Using our texts and lessons on inventors, write a script in which these historical figures would discuss their inventions. Choose a character and role play this scenario, thinking about what your inventor would say about the other inventions and about how his invention impacted society.

In the third example, students must take information they have learned and go beyond the knowledge gained to internalize the information and use it in another format. Students are stepping into a role-play scenario, using evidence and reasoning to generate hypothetical conversation between people with opposing viewpoints while maintaining the essence of the person's true personality. Finally, they are taking the knowledge about each of the persons and applying it to a current situation. This also requires them to move beyond the text, which in this case is what they have learned. With younger learners, consider role play through discussion and seminar without a written script. While this assignment uses inventors, it could easily be used with characters from a novel.

Example Four: Exploring a Theme in Grades 4–5

After reading a series of picture books/short stories or poems on friendship, determine common themes that seem to recur. Create a parallel chart or semantic feature analysis of four of the texts, noting commonalities and differences in plot, characters, conflict, etc. Write a brief analysis of each story/poem, concluding with an overarching theme that connects them. Justify your ideas with textual evidence from the texts.

Finally, decide how this theme is present in your own life. As the protagonist in your own story, to what degree are you learning this life lesson?

In example four, students are asked to make connections across several literary texts and identify a theme that appears in each of the stories (nonfiction, fiction, and poetry). They must develop a rationale for their chosen theme by using textual evidence from each story. Finally, they go beyond the text by applying this theme to their own life and determining whether they are learning from the wisdom in the theme. This could also be easily adapted to social studies with any topic that involves themes.

Example Five: Varying Perspectives

We have been reading and talking about the adventures of Tum Tum and Nutmeg. Living in a world where everything is considerably larger than them, we see their unique perspective on places and events that are ordinary to us. Being "small" in your own world, how can you connect with these mice? Are there times when you wish you were bigger or older or that your voice was heard more clearly? Are there times when you "see" things differently than the adults around you? What would you say to the adults in your life about the way you see things?

Now let's read *Clifford, the Big Red Dog*. How is Clifford's view of the world very different than Emily Elizabeth's? What's different about seeing things from a much larger point of view? Imagine that you have been sent to a deserted island where everything is very, very small. Your view of the world would be quite different than the little people that live there. Using pictures and/or words, describe how you might see things from a different perspective.

In this particular example, Aldyn Keefer, a first grade teacher in Charlotte, North Carolina, reads various *Tum Tum and Nutmeg* books with her students. To enrich their understanding and help students move to deeper levels of thinking, she first has them think about how the mice see things from a different perspective. She then asks them to connect this to their lives by asking them to think about times when they see things differently than the adults around them, and to consider telling them how they view the world around them. Finally, she asks them to change perspectives and imagine being larger than their surroundings (much like *Clifford, the Big Red Dog*). Students must put themselves in another character's shoes to consider life from a different angle.

Projects, Project-Based Learning, and Problem-Based Learning

Do you remember doing projects when you were a student? We do. Our teachers typically assigned everyone a standard project; we completed them and turned them in and then received a grade. It wasn't very rigorous. Today, teachers use standard projects, project-based learning, and problem-based learning. Let's look at how they compare.

Projects, Project-Based Learning, and Problem-Based Learning		
Projects	*Project-Based Learning*	*Problem-Based Learning*
♦ Finished product is the focus. ♦ Teacher works mainly after the project is complete. ♦ Based on directions and are done "like last year." ♦ Are oftentimes done at home (hopefully independently by the student). ♦ Are closed; every project has the same goal (such as create a diorama of a scene from the novel).	♦ Student involvement is the focus. ♦ Teacher works mainly before the project starts, although some support is provided to students who need it. ♦ Are relevant to students' lives or future lives. ♦ Are based on driving questions developed by the teacher that encompass the learning and establish the need to know. ♦ Are open ended; students make choices that determine the outcome and path of the research.	♦ Student inquiry is the focus. ♦ Are based on driving questions developed by students. ♦ Are open ended; students make choices that determine the outcome and path of the research. ♦ Project is student directed, with the teacher providing support as needed but typically in a guidance role.

Source: Adapted from a blog entry by Terry Heick at teachthought.com.

Project-based and problem-based learning are more rigorous than a standard project, in part because more responsibility and ownership is shifted to students. Additionally, project- and problem-based learning usually requires a more advanced level of thinking.

The following three assignments might be options for students. Notice the differences between the project assignment, the project-based assignment, and the problem-based assignment.

English/Language Arts		
Project	*Project-Based Learning*	*Problem-Based Learning*
Create a shadow box scene from the story we've read in class. Make sure the details included accurately represent the setting of the book. In your presentation to the class, explain why you chose this scene and how the story would have been different if this scene would have been omitted.	Roald Dahl used well-developed characters in his story *Charlie and the Chocolate Factory*. Think about each of the four naughty children, the way they misbehaved, and how their behavior caused them to exit the factory earlier than they anticipated (in very odd ways). Create a new character with a different behavior problem and write him or her into the story. How would this character treat his or her parent and others? What would he or she look like and what would their mannerisms be? What would get him or her into trouble during his tour of the chocolate factory that would lead to him or her getting "thrown out"? How would the existing characters react/respond to this new character? Finally, become this new character, introducing yourself to our class in the way the character would act in the book and tell us of your experience in the chocolate factory. Use details from the setting and plot to weave in your own story and step into character!	Our class has no field trips planned this year! Given the units we will be studying, think about the opportunities around our city and state that could make learning come to life for us. You could choose a location or a series of locations. In your small group, develop a research plan for discovering what our area has to offer. Be creative and think outside the box. Be sure to answer the following questions in your field trip proposal: What would we do on this trip? What/who would we see? How would it be an extension of our learning? Write a short persuasive letter or speech to convince the principal that our class would benefit greatly from going on the field trip you are proposing! Justify your ideas by referring to the goals for our units and the added value of an out-of-class experience.

In the first project assignment, students are primarily tasked with re-creating a scene visually in a different format. Comprehension of the text and some level of analysis is required to complete the project but is solely based on assessing understanding of the text. There is very little rigor involved with this project.

For the project-based assignment, students are taking what they've read and creating a new character to be woven into the plot. Students must visualize what the character would look like, how the existing characters would respond to this new character, and determine what would lead to the character's downfall.

In the problem-based learning assignment, students are informed about a problem that exists in their own community. They must decide how to research and gather evidence related to this issue as well as ideas for improving it. Finally, they must propose their own solution and steps to accomplish it and present it to a committee of adults. This problem uses a real-life scenario as a catalyst for further student-driven learning.

Social Studies		
Project	*Project-Based Learning*	*Problem-Based Learning*
Design a brochure to visit one of the seven continents we've explored. Use blank computer paper or construction paper for your final product. Be sure to include pictures and details about famous landmarks, climates, and geological features. Finally, develop a one-line slogan that will persuade us to visit your continent.	As we've studied, archeologists and how they excavate bones have taught us about dinosaurs of the past. Archeologists also have other goals to uncover our history as a people. Let's extend our learning by completing research. Continue to gather more information about archeologists by exploring other types of work they do. Choose one other field in which they work from the list provided and teach the class about it. Be sure to include where this work takes place, what type of work it involves, what they hope to accomplish in the near future with their project, and how they will use this discovery to impact us. After listening to and charting all of our classmates' discoveries, we will have a debate about which of the projects/goals seem to be the most important to understanding our past.	The city is in danger. The mayor has moved and everything has shut down! We have been asked to design a plan to get the city up and running. Think about all of the critical roles we've discussed in creating an effective community. In your small groups, complete research and determine how you would propose we help out as efficiently as possible. Justify your ideas with textual evidence and logical reasoning. Your final product will be a persuasive visual presentation using chart paper, PowerPoint, poster board, handout, etc. that outlines your proposal with information about your plan and pictures, graphs, maps, etc. You'll also write a justification for your plan, explaining why it is the best option for rebuilding the city.

Notice again that in the problem-based learning examples, students drive the topic. Although general guidelines are provided, they determine how they will research and present the topic provided. That said, there are various ways to integrate technology into your classroom when designing and implementing PBLs. The following resources may be valuable ways to connect twenty-first-century skills to this type of assignment.

Technology Resources

Novare PBL Platform is a project management tool which uses narratives, portfolios, and learning goals to structure project-based learning.

Prezi incorporates video, audio, and other interactive research components for a presentation that keeps everyone's attention.

Project Foundry is a popular learning tool that enables students to plan their own learning and track their progress. It also makes organizing student projects much easier for students and teachers. Schools also love that Project Foundry gives students the chance to build digital portfolios – a necessary skill in today's evolving technological culture.

Scribble Press allows students options to share the work they've done with others while reflecting on the experience as a whole. Scribble Press allows students to write and illustrate their own books, as well as retelling the story of their challenge-based experience, include final project results, and reflect on moments of personal growth.

In what follows, we've provided additional resources on project-based and problem-based learning. Remember, check the information to be sure it moves beyond simple projects so that the level of rigor in your assignments increases.

Resources for Project-Based and Problem-Based Learning

Buck Institute for Education

www.bie.org/about/what_pbl

Project-based learning resources for teachers such as blogs, videos, and links to resources for projects

Edutopia

www.edutopia.org/project-based-learning

Tips for using project-based learning in math and other articles like increasing student engagement with project-based learning

TeachThought

www.teachthought.com/category/project-based-learning/

Examples of project-based learning activities, how to avoid pitfalls of PBL and ideas for differentiating project-based learning

www.cultofpedagogy.com/project-based-learning/

Tried-and-true PBL ideas from an educator's perspective

Problem-Based Learning: Six Steps to Design, Implement, and Assess, Vincent R. Genareo, PhD, and Renee Lyons, *Faculty Focus*

Practical PBL Series: Design an Instructional Unit in Seven Phases, Amber Graeber, *Edutopia*

Genius Hour

Genius Hour is an excellent way to enhance problem-based learning. Genius Hour is inspired by Google's efforts with its employees, where 20% of employees' time is motivated by passion and curiosity. They found that their employees were happier, more creative, and more productive. Educators have adapted this for use in a classroom, shifting to the concept of providing students one hour to work on their passions. When we apply this with students and allow them freedom to design their own learning and explore their own interests, it increases an intrinsic sense of purpose. Many schools are now implementing Genius Hour, which occurs for a minimum of one hour per week. Key principles of genius hours are that students take charge of their own learning, including the design of the task, use of inquiry to navigate learning and the creation of a finished product to demonstrate a deep understanding of their topics.

However, some common mistakes can derail a successful Genius Hour experience for your students.

Common Mistakes

- Allowing total choice without providing guidance and support (some structure is needed, particularly as they work on their projects)
- Assuming you aren't teaching during Genius Hour (you are teaching in a different way, as a facilitator of learning)
- Forgetting to leave time for processing and reflection (critical to success; this also includes feedback from others and you)
- Not providing the opportunity to practice the final presentation
- Assuming young learners aren't capable

Genius Hour Based on Students' Interests

Inherent in the philosophy of a Genius Hour is the notion that students' topics are driven by things they value. Although you want to give students the widest latitude possible to choose their topics, you may need to provide some guidance, especially for students who are less ready for independent work. In the K–5 classroom, consider reading the picture book *What Do You Do With an Idea?* by Kobi Yamada. This simple story demonstrates how a simple thought or question can grow and grow into a beautiful idea if nurtured and given the time to bloom. In a perfect world, your students will develop their own ideas, but you may want to give them some topics to use as a starting point. Begin by having younger students keep track of their wonder questions (you could chart these as a class over a period of time). Kindergarten students could draw a picture about something they are interested in and then begin to develop questions about it. Terry Heick of TeachThought PD suggests using variations of the Question Formula Technique (QFT) to facilitate the question-making process for students, as Genius Hour is based on the concept of students answering their own natural questions with research.

Question Formula Technique

Dan Rothstein and Luz Santana, in their book *Make Just One Change: Teach Students to Ask Their Own Questions*, describe a process for students to develop questions. The Question Formulation Technique (QFT) teaches students to follow six steps.

QFT Steps	
Step	*Description*
Step One: Question Focus	A stimulus or springboard you will use to ask questions. Can be a topic, image, phrase or situation that will serve as the "focus" for generating questions.
Step Two: Producing Questions	Ask as many questions as you can. Don't stop to discuss, judge, or answer. Write down every question exactly as it is stated. Change any statement into a question.
Step Three: Improving Questions	Analyze and identify your questions as open or closed ended. Discuss the value of each and practice changing questions from one type to another.
Step Four: Prioritizing Questions	Select your top-priority questions based on your learning goals. Name a rationale for your prioritization and notice where it comes in the process.
Step Five: Next Steps	Your questions can now be put into action. What will you do with them? How will you work to answer them?
Step Six: Reflection	Reflect on the work you have done: what you have learned and how you can use it. The reflection helps internalize the process, its value and how to apply it further.

You will likely need to provide structure and support for Genius Hour. The amount and type of scaffolding will depend on the readiness levels of your students. Some students may need more prompting to begin their brainstorming. Here are some generic ideas you may use to get them started. Even if the original response is a science-based idea, they still need to use literacy and research skills to discover the answers!

QuestionsThat Can Ignite Creativity

- Have you ever wondered how something works or how it was made? Let's research it and find out!
- Could you imagine creating a world or storyline from a character in one of your video games? Try writing and/or illustrating your own story!
- What would happen if. . . ?
- What are your big "why" questions?

The teachers we talked with provided several sample topics their students have completed.

Sample Topics for Elementary LA/SS

Fundraising for a Local Cause

Random Acts of Kindness

Teach Others to Care for Animals

Planets

How to Hit a Home Run

Planning a Community Park

Teaching How to Play a Game

Designing a New Country

About Me

Symbols of the United States (or your state)

Once students have chosen a topic, they give an "elevator pitch," which is a 3-minute talk proposing the idea. They can present this to other students or to you. They can use feedback from the teacher and students to adjust their proposals. Some students will be able to complete this with no additional guidelines. Others may need a graphic organizer to help them plan, and for others, you may need to provide small-group coaching.

Guiding Questions for Genius Hour Feedback

- What is the overall question you are answering?
- What have you done/where are you in the process?
- What has changed since you started/since we last talked?
- What help do you need from me?
- Is there anything else I should know?

The process of investigation is similar, with some students navigating their own learning and others needing some level of guidance and support from you, whether in the form of recommended resources, structured study guides, or small-group instruction. The following technology resources may aid in this process.

Technology Resources

Kiddle (www.kiddle.co) is a Google search engine developed especially for kids. With visual thumbnails and large Arial font, all search results must meet family-friendly requirements that have been handpicked by kiddle editors.

Wonderopolis (wonderopolis.org) posts wonder questions daily, with researched answers students can listen to with the included audio feature. Some wonder answers are accompanied with a video as well; both features are ideal for emergent readers. Students can also ask their own wonders!

Wizard School is an app for ipads or Andriods that inspires creativity in very young learners. Formerly known as Wonderbox, the content, developed by educators, contains over three thousand videos, maps, and other content to help students investigate topics of interest. The creators of the app recently partnered with Khan Academy to create a safe learning environment for children around the world.

Educurious is a website with supplemental apps that aims to turn students into "developing experts" by connecting them with real-world mentors.

Ed.VoiceThread is a platform where students develop critical thinking, communication, collaboration, and creativity skills.

The Knowledge Compass helps students formulate questions and begin the research process. The website provides several different types of questions to help students ask the right questions to guide their research.

For the final product, all students need the opportunity to practice their presentations. The presentation of the end product also requires varying levels of support based on students' readiness. Interestingly, you may have students who are quite advanced in designing and investigating a topic but who struggle with the final product. Remember that students' readiness or skill levels can change at different stages. That's why formative assessment, which we will address in Chapter 6, is critical.

Genius Hour in the Elementary Classroom

Some teachers question whether or not Genius Hour is appropriate in the elementary school. Meshelle Smith, a fifth grade teacher, provides a perspective for Edutopia readers who are teaching the elementary grades (www.edutopia.org/article/genius-hour-elementary-school). She describes her goal of teaching students who demonstrate creativity, curiosity, and intellectual development, as well as how she structured her classroom to ensure students would have those opportunities. As she explains, "Genius Hour could be adapted to any grade level or student type. This year I plan on expanding it to my special education class. The vibrant creativity pulls students into the learning process and makes school a place they want to be – and that's not exclusive to one age or type of student."

However, there is still the question of primary students, who may have minimal or limited literacy skills. Denise Krebs, in a blog on geniushourguide.org, shares comments from primary teachers using Genius Hour in their classrooms (www.geniushourguide.org/genius-hour-in-the-primary-classroom/). They provide excellent pointers for primary teachers, such as using PebbleGo, a paid program that reads to teachers, utilizing Kiddle (a kid's search engine with all items vetted by Google Certified teachers), and teaming up with older students or adult volunteers.

Conclusion

We often think that high expectations start with our standards. But our behavior toward students is really the starting point. Then we need to look at criteria for rigorous expectations and samples of tasks and assignments that meet the criteria and provide opportunities for students to respond to high expectations through activities such as projects, project-based learning, problem-based learning and Genius Hour.

Points to Ponder

- The most important thing learned. . .
- One strategy I want to implement now . . .
- One strategy I want to save for later. . .
- I'd like to learn more about. . .
- I'd like to share with other teachers. . .

4

Support and Scaffolding

Many teachers think that the rigor has been "watered down" if we need to support a student in a complex activity. When we ask students to work at rigorous levels, it's critical to provide scaffolding that is intentional and purposeful. Many students are not willing or ready to think critically and deeply unless prompted to do so. Even then, they may not know how to take surface-level thoughts and make them more abstract, creative or complex. When some students perceive that a task is overwhelming or difficult, they shut down before even beginning. This is where we help them utilize tools and strategies that will guide them through a mentally challenging academic task. Supporting students and teaching them to approach complex thinking with more confidence and grit will allow all students to access rigorous curriculum. Though the term has evolved over the past few decades, the essence of the word remains the same: teachers provide temporary learning tools or employ purposeful strategies in progressive stages of student learning, with a gradual release of independence.

How Do I Provide Scaffolding For My Students?

The outdated practice of assigning and assessing with little to no instruction in between is ineffective. Students learn from their mistakes, and whether you're teaching writing with first graders or teaching a fifth grade social studies lesson, those in-the-moment lessons are the ones that stick with students. Though there are numerous methods for scaffolding, we're going to focus on five key areas.

Five Areas

- Teaching through modeling
- Utilizing visual literacy
- Creating a toolbox of strategies
- Deepening understanding
- Working with special populations

Modeling

It's important to show students "what good looks like." If you never provide students a glimpse into where your expectations are set, students are trying to hit a target blindfolded. Three types of modeling are helpful: modeling a finished product, modeling reading, and modeling writing.

Modeling a Finished Product

When students are asked to complete a task or assignment, it's important to show them a model of your expectations for a finished product. When asking students to complete a graphic story that summarizes Paul Revere's ride or *The Island of the Blue Dolphins*, you might start by showing them an exemplary version of the same product from a different historical event or different novel. In grades K–2, consider putting pictures in sequence for *Clifford, the Big Red Dog* before asking students to do it with another picture book you read as a class. This may be time consuming the first time you integrate a new project, as you do not have student samples in your repertoire. However, having a visual example that includes the level of artistic detail and textual evidence you're expecting will help students work at a more rigorous level. In reality, most students do not spontaneously choose to complete their assignments at a high level, so we must show them how to think deeply rather than skimming the surface of an assignment. Don't make them guess what you're looking for; rather, encourage them to take what you've shown them and think of creative, even better ways to complete the task. Students' thoughts will become more complex if you set the standard first.

Modeling Reading

Students often need assistance with reading text. A Guide-O-Rama guides the students through an assigned text, providing support so they can read and learn at more rigorous levels. Used by students as they read, a Guide-O-Rama is different from a regular outline or study guide in that it takes students by the hand and walks them through the text. It's the next best thing to actually sitting down with a student and reading the text with them. The Guide-O-Rama is almost like a think-aloud written down on paper for the student.

How to Build a Guide-O-Rama

1. Identify a chunk of content you need students to read. Guide-O-Ramas should be used with challenging texts that you anticipate students will struggle with.
2. Determine guiding questions that will help them process key portions of the text, similar to what you would use in a traditional study guide.
3. Add think-aloud comments, such as, "Notice that on page 56, there is a key that explains what the map symbols represent. When I see a box of text in the margin of the text, I pay special attention since it usually contains important information." These are typically statements and/or questions that you would verbally use to model your thinking for students.
4. Use visuals that will help students remember the content. For example, if students are learning about the characteristics of two countries, give them a graphic organizer that has outlines of the two countries rather than a simple chart.
5. Keep in mind that your goal is twofold: help students process and understand the complex text and move toward independence in learning.

The following is an example of a Guide-O-Rama that could be used with a fourth or fifth grade level social studies textbook.

Guide-O-Rama *The Original Thirteen Colonies Face Problems – Chpt. 6 (Sections 6.1–6.2)*	
Page #	*Reading Tip*
124–128	Look at the map provided. I bet the location of Great Britain impacted its involvement in the colonies. This might be something I want to watch for in the text as I read.
129	There are so many reasons why the colonies wanted to separate from Great Britain, but they are scattered throughout the next several pages. I think it would be helpful to keep track of them all in one place. Let's make a two-column box to bullet point them as we notice them in the text.
130–139	As I read this section, I immediately see bolded terms that look unfamiliar: nationalism, colonialism, and monarchy. I need to see how these terms relate to pre–Revolutionary War days and how they differ. I'm certainly going to add these to my notes!
140–143	There seem to be a lot of dates and "acts" on these pages. As I read this section, I'm going to make a timeline of the different taxes and acts imposed on the colonies and their reaction to them.
144	I found it interesting that spies were used in the war! Who do you think might be willing to be a spy for Great Britain?
148	There seem to be multiple factors that contributed to the signing of the Declaration of Independence. Some seem to be more significant than others. I think I'll rank them in order of significance.

We've found that written Guide-O-Ramas are effective beginning at second grade, and oral versions work well with PK–1 students. If you think the Guide-O-Rama is too complex for your students, cut the steps apart. Students receive the first step/slip of paper and follow the directions. When they finish, they show you the work and receive the next step. Follow the process until they complete the work, and you have chunked the information for students along with modeling. As a bonus, many students think they are completing a treasure hunt, which can improve motivation.

Modeling Writing

Similarly, students must have mentor texts to study and deconstruct as they begin to build knowledge of style and format of a particular mode of writing. When asking students to write a personal narrative or a point of view paragraph, we must first show them what sound elements of that mode actually looks like. You may choose a well-written mentor text that visibly includes the structure and elements of what you're expecting from students. But don't stop there. Allow students to deconstruct this mentor text, isolating the "ingredients" of that mode of writing. As they locate the elements and not the organizational structure, students will begin to understand how the elements tie together seamlessly to create a text. Color-coding the various parts of a text may help visual learners!

How to Choose a Mentor Text

- Are the elements of the text mode clearly recognizable?
- Is the level of reading accessible to students at an independent level?
- Does the organizational structure of the mentor text resemble the structure you would like your students to emulate?
- Is the text concise enough for students to remain focused on structure and elements?
- Is the text content appropriate for your students?

A quick Google search can provide a list of excellent picture books/short stories/poems that could serve as a mentor text for whatever element you want students to see.

	Mentor Text for K–2	*Mentor Text for 3–5*
Onomatopoeia, personification	♦ *We're Going on a Bear Hunt* by Helen Oxenbury ♦ *Squeak, Rumble, Whomp! Whomp! Whomp!: A Sonic Adventure* by Wynton Marsalis and Paul Rogers	♦ *Why Mosquitoes Buzz in People's Ears* by Verna Aardema and Leo Dillon ♦ *With the Fire on High* by Elizabeth Acevedo
Sensory details	♦ *All the Way to Havana* by Margarita Engle and Mike Curato ♦ *Good night, laila tov* by Laurel Snyder	♦ *My Mama Had a Dancing Heart* by Libba Gray ♦ *Serafina's Promise* by Ann E. Burg
Strong character	♦ *Islandborn* by Junot Diaz	♦ *All Summer in a Day* by Ray Bradbury
Word choice	♦ *The Word Collector* by Peter Reynolds	♦ *Water Dance* by Thomas Locker

A next step would be to help students who need additional scaffolding by breaking this process down for them. Show them what it looks like to brainstorm through possible topics and hooks. Choose one of your own, and walk through each step of writing the hook, brainstorming details to include, drafting sentences, etc. This should be done in a "watch me, then you try" fashion – one step at a time as needed. How do you manage this in a class of thirty students? Group students by ability. Hold mini-writing conferences that are tailored for the readiness level of each group. I may announce at the beginning of class that the goal for the day is to draft a topic sentence, and since anyone may need a refresher on how to do this, I will be reviewing over by the windows. Others who feel competent in this area can get started with the resources they've been given. This provides a way to invite students to seek scaffolding from you before they begin the writing task. After holding a writing conference, it may be helpful to give the student(s) cue cards with specific "take aways" and guidelines you discussed.

Sample Mini-Writing Conferences for Support

- Selecting a topic
- Brainstorming details
- Choosing and writing a hook
- Writing a topic sentence
- Organizing evidence in logical manner
- Writing a conclusion

Visual Literacy

Our students are visual learners. Our society, as a whole, is becoming more and more reliant on the information we can see, such as infographics, virtual marketing, and augmented reality. In order to best reach our students, we must be prepared to make information more visual if the complexity of text is impeding a student's learning process. Using graphics to organize and make sense of written information is a strategy we would hope becomes inherent to each learner.

Graphic Organizers

Graphic organizers have been a tried-and-true tool for educators for years by helping students make overwhelming information more visual and understandable. Each has its own specific purpose and should be chosen strategically to accomplish the learning goal. What we don't often consider is that you can make your own graphic organizer for any areas in which your students are having trouble thinking at a rigorous level. For example, when middle school language arts students are trying to determine the plot of a short story or novel, the following visual may help guide their thoughts.

I Can Re-tell A Story in My Own Words!!		
Main character(s):		
Beginning details	Middle details	Ending details
Lesson the main character learned:		

In contrast, perhaps an upper level elementary school history standard asks students to explain multiple causes and effects of events and developments in the past. To best help students who may need scaffolding for this assignment, you may choose to provide an adaptation of the following graphic organizer as they unpack the causes and effects of the signing of the Declaration of Independence.

Adapted Graphic Organizer

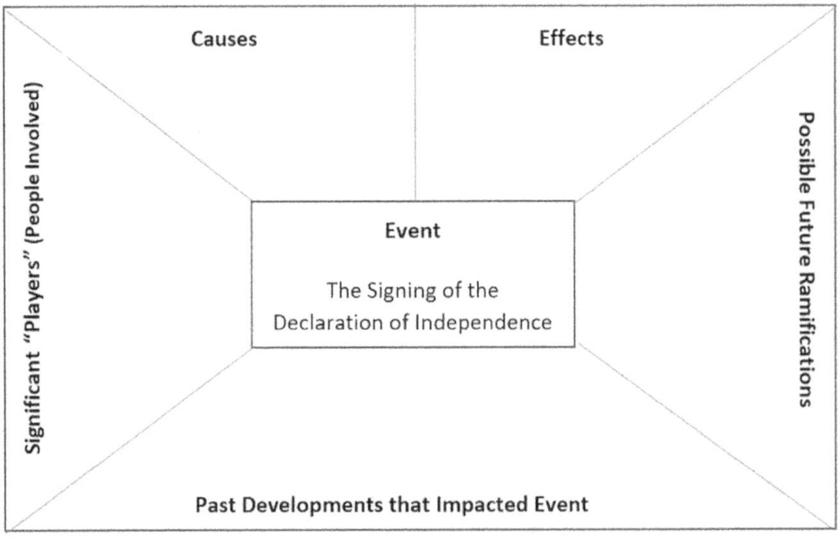

A semantic feature analysis also creates a visual for students trying to synthesize information from multiple texts. It helps them look for patterns and make connections while acquiring a deeper comprehension of the text. In a second grade language arts lesson, I may have students analyze the differences and similarities between creation myths A common state standard for second grade asks students to recount stories, including fables and folktales from diverse cultures, and determine common characteristics and morals (themes). This activity allows deeper conversation within each group as they analyze various creation stories from different cultures, but it also requires collaboration between groups to compare and contrast various beliefs in how the world came into existence. Students must make inferences, draw conclusions, and discern an understanding of the genre at large as they contemplate many different perspectives and belief systems.

Grades 3–5 Semantic Feature Analysis Chart for Creation Myth Across Cultures

	How the World Began?	*Creator?*	*First Human?*	*First Animals?*
Iroquois				
Greek				
African Bushmen				
Chinese				

Grades K–2 Semantic Feature Analysis Chart for Fables			
	Are the Characters Animals?	*Lesson Learned? (Moral)*	*Trickster?*
The Tortoise and the Hare			
The Boy Who Cried Wolf			
The Lion and the Mouse			

Note: This would be a great idea for an anchor chart as students familiarize themselves with the elements of fables.

Grades 3–5 Semantic Feature Analysis Chart for a Unit on Westward Expansion			
	Inventor	*Purpose*	*Historical Impact*
Railroads			
Steel plow			
Cotton gin			
Steam engine			
Telegraph			

Other Visual Support Strategies

Aside from graphic organizers, there are other ways to make reading and writing more visual for our students. Anytime you sense that perhaps more support is needed to help them access the text or concepts you are teaching, consider making the information visual before leading them back to the text and ultimate goal.

Other Ways to Make Reading and Writing More Visual	
Text/Concept	*Visualization Strategy*
The Battle of Bunker Hill in history	Reenact the battle using balled-up paper as the ammunition: assign significant characters and quotes
Understanding sequencing in *The True Story of the Three Little Pigs* (or any story)	Allow students to become frozen/wax statues representing the characters and "pose" the scenes

Other Ways to Make Reading and Writing More Visual	
Text/Concept	*Visualization Strategy*
Essay or paragraph writing (any mode of writing)	Use color-coded sticky notes to collect textual evidence, research, etc. for each paragraph. The sticky notes can then be rearranged to determine logical progression of ideas within the paragraph before it is written.
Understanding propaganda in media and history	View several commercials, billboards, and/or pop-up ads and discuss how they are trying to persuade you.
Understanding where quotations and punctuation go when using dialogue	Have students become words and punctuation marks in a sentence by holding signs and determine where they should stand in a given sentence.

Creating a Toolbox

Obviously, we will not be with our students forever, so they must have the tools necessary to be independent thinkers and learners. Our job is to equip them for this by teaching strategies that can eventually be self-selected. The use of instructional strategies allows students to access texts and tasks that may seem too complex at first glance. Teachers are typically well versed in using strategies with our students, but here's where we fall short: We fail to name them with intentionality and explain to our students why we have chosen to use a specific tool to help them. How will they be able to decide which strategy to use on their own if we haven't taught them how to select an appropriate tool to unlock meaning or aid in completion of an assignment?

There are many resources with suggested tools to help students unlock the meaning of texts or work through a challenging writing task in order to integrate strategies into daily learning. The following chart is a sampling of these effective strategies. Again, the goal is to teach students to use the strategies independently when they encounter rigorous material. After using them with intentionality in your classroom, begin to coach students to utilize them on their own by asking them which strategy they think could be applied instead of doing it for them.

Student Strategies		
Strategy	*Definition*	*Purpose*
Chunking the Text	Separating the text into smaller, more manageable sections and setting a purpose for each chunk	To reduce the intimidation factor when encountering long words, sentences or whole texts; to increase comprehension of difficult or challenging text
Marking the Text	Using predetermined markers to interact with the text (i.e., a smiley face for something that excites you, a heart for something you love, a frowny face for text that makes you sad, etc.)	To focus reading for specific purposes and make reading an active process rather than passive

Choral Read	Students read a piece of text together or with the teacher	To increase fluency in reading
Sketching the Text	Students visualize what a scene looks like and sketch it beside the text	Another way of visualizing, this helps ensure that students are making a movie in their mind as they read
Task Cards	Using cards to outline single, clear tasks to be completed individually, as a group, or at a station	Task cards will keep students focused and create independence during the learning process
Mapping	Creating a graphic organizer that serves as a visual representation of the organizational plan for a written text	To generate ideas, concepts, or key words that provide a focus and/or establish organization during the prewriting, drafting or revision process
Think-Pair-Share	Students are given time to think about their response to a question before pairing up with a partner to discuss their ideas, and lastly, sharing combined ideas with the larger group	This strategy allows time for each student to individually process a question and gather thoughts before discussing with others

Remember, every student will not need every strategy in a given lesson. The beauty of scaffolding is that teachers can choose which strategies to use with a student as they anticipate where they may need assistance or as they notice a learner hitting a roadblock. Familiarity with the strategies will allow you to access them quickly for your students, and their level of comfort with them will allow them to pull them out of their box of tools as needed to access rigorous material in other courses.

Deepening Understanding

Many of the scaffolding techniques mentioned previously help students deepen understanding, but let's discuss some other intentional ways to help them look beyond the surface level of a task or text.

Flesh It Out

Let's look at a fun visual to help students go deeper with a topic. Flesh It Out, originally created by Janet Allen, requires an analysis of a prominent historical figure or character in a novel. Rather than simply writing basic information about a person or character, students are expected to research and describe more specific information, which allows them to create a finished product with more complexity.

Flesh It Out Social Studies

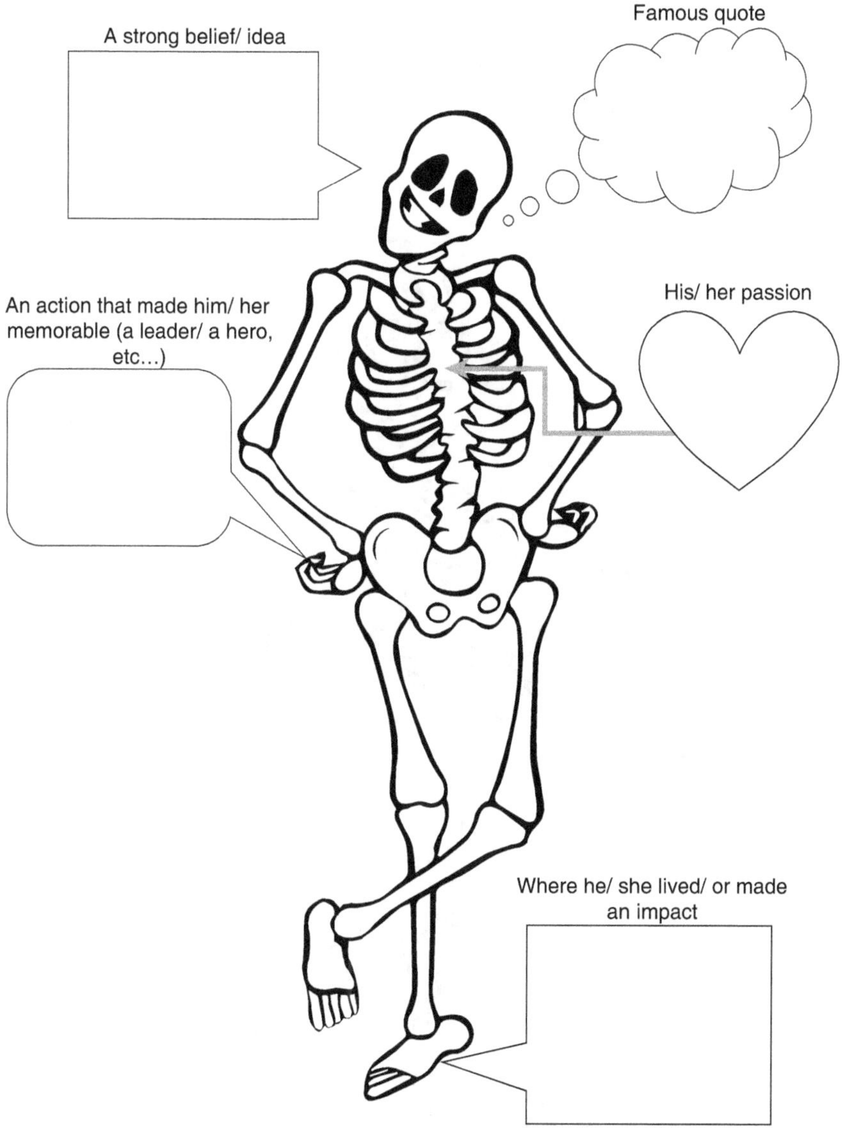

If used in a lesson after reading a story, this same tool could be used to help students with character analysis by simply changing the headings of the elements. You may want students to understand more about one of the characters by recording important spoken words of the main character, the actions, the time/place in which he or she lived, a significant decision or choice he or she made, or how he or she made a difference in the lives of others. After taking time to flesh out the subtleties, students can look at the full characterization to gain a more complex understanding of the character.

Flesh It Out ELA

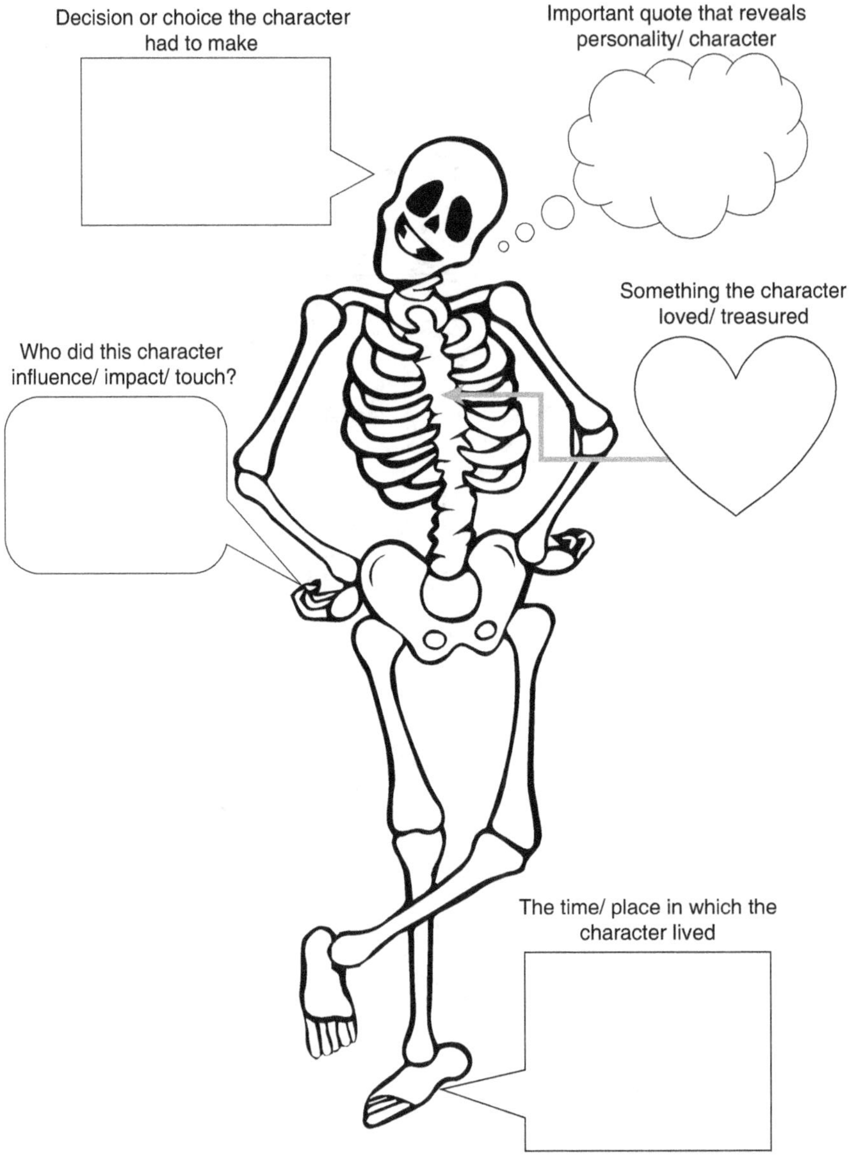

Role Play

Another way students can gain deeper meaning is by experiencing the event or topic firsthand through role play and experiential learning.

When learning about archeology, you could allow students to experience an archeological dig using a sandbox or sensory table filled with sand and buried treasures. Martha Thorne, a teacher in North Carolina, would allow her students to experience the process of mummification with chickens that she bought and brought into class. Second graders could benefit from a simulation of a New England colony, in which each student was assigned a role to play. Regardless of the subject matter, students are making history come to life as they interact with it during class.

Simulations can also be done with literature. In a first grade class, students can make the story *The Goggle-Eyed Goats* come to life by staging it and acting out the narrative. Assign a narrator (or two or three), students choose to role play Al Haji Amadu, each wife and daughter, goats, and a narrator. Carefully listening as the story is read aloud, each student steps into his or her assigned character and acts out the events that unfold, turning your classroom into the Sahel region of West Africa! This could work with narrative poems, such as *Casey at the Bat*, or short stories as well.

Having students experience each of these settings allows them to acquire a deeper, more intimate understanding of the concept than if they had simply read about the subject matter.

You can help your students visualize almost anything in the social studies and ELA classrooms, no matter the age or level of the student. Think outside the box and turn written text into an activity your students can see and experience!

Repeated Readings

Kindergarten and first grade teachers realize the power of building fluency with multiple reads of a text, but we seem to veer from this practice as students get older. However, all students need opportunities to reread text to gain deeper meaning with each read. Several close reading strategies exist to help students access deeper meaning from a text. Many of these strategies are utilized in Advanced Placement courses, but research shows that they are useful to all students at much younger ages, so numerous variations have been created. When doing a close reading with students, multiple readings of the text are required, as the first time read will most likely only result in surface-level comprehension. However, with guidance and knowledge of how to read more closely by analyzing certain features of the text, students can reach a much deeper understanding. You may consider creating an anchor chart to remind students of the tasks to complete during each read.

Close Reading Principle	*Things to Consider*
Multiple reads	Whether the teacher is doing all of the readings in grades K–2, the students are doing all reads independently, or there's a strategic balance of both (i.e., student reads the first time, teacher reads aloud the second time), it is imperative to read a text that is complex multiple times.
Limit frontloading	Part of the close read is to teach students to gather information in steps. As the teacher, you want students to grapple a bit with comprehension to push them to their outer zone of proximity. Sometimes it's crucial to let students see what they figure out without too much preteaching.
Text selections	Close readings work with texts that are short enough to manage with multiple reads. Depth over breadth is emphasized with short reads. The reading level should be just beyond your students' independent reading level.
Set a purpose for each read	The purpose for a first read may simply be to monitor understanding and make meaning of the text (basic comprehension), whereas for the second read, you ask students to pay close attention to a specific aspect in the text. Still yet, the third read may require students to move into grade-appropriate analysis of character or choices/consequences, cause/effect, etc. Directing them to mark the text with specific markers (!, *, ?) during reading will help students remain focused on the purpose you have given them for that particular read.
Text-dependent questions	It is important to create well-written questions that will guide students after their first read of a text. These questions should remand that students reread in order to fully respond. It is also critical that the question categories vary (i.e., questions should require students to think about comprehension, analysis, author's style, vocabulary, inferences, textual connections, etc.)

Paired Texts

Pairing texts allows students to see the same concept or topic from different perspectives, in different genres, which is more rigorous than simply looking at a standard text. A broader sense of understanding will begin to take shape as various authors and media formats are presented.

Sample Paired Texts			
Grade/ Subject	***Primary Text***	***Paired Written Text***	***Paired Non-Print/ Primary Source Text***
Third grade Social Studies	*Harriet Tubman: Conductor on the Underground Railroad* by Ann Petry	Picture book: *The Last Safe House* by Barbara Greenwood	Clips from a video documentary *Unchained Memories: Readings from the Slave Narratives;* song "Follow the Drinking Gourd"
Fifth grade Social Studies	Social Studies textbook	Picture book: *The Gardner* by Sarah Stewart	Primary source document: Pictures from the Great Depression from the Library of Congress
K–1 Citizenship	*Nonfiction: What Can a Citizen Do?* by Dave Eggers	*Fiction: The Red Bicycle* by Jude Isabella	Film: Family Education Series *– Being A Good Citizen*
Fourth Grade: Changes	*Short Story: Eleven* by Sandra Cisneros	Poem: *Advice From a Caterpillar* by Rachel Rooney	Movie clip: *The Lion King* (where Simba is afraid to go back to the Pride Lands

Many free online resources also offer ideas for paired texts. Try utilizing the paired text sets at CommonLit.org, Readworks.org, or Zinc Learning Labs to help your students deepen their understanding.

Emphasize Good Reading Habits

Many of the leading researchers of reading instruction agree that strong readers apply certain core habits when making meaning of text. Though the wording may vary between experts, they are essentially the same: questioning the text, determining what's important, making inferences and predictions, visualizing, monitoring for meaning, activating prior knowledge, and synthesizing information. It is important, whether teaching kindergarten or fifth grade or anything in between, to model these habits routinely so that students begin to use them naturally with texts they read or listen to.

Seven Habits of Strong Readers	
Questioning the Text	Teach students to constantly question what they're reading. When actively engaging with text, students should be naturally wondering "Why are the boys on Mars?", "Who could be the man behind the door?", "What does eager mean?", "Will the horse ever be free?" and other such questions. This inquisitive nature will build interest and suspense as students encounter new texts for the first time.
Determining Importance	Teachers model, through think-alouds and discussions, how to determine the most important events/details in a text. It is oftentimes difficult for students of all ages to filter through extraneous details to really zoom in on the main idea and author's purpose for a written text.
Making Inferences/ Predictions	Students must be trained to pick up on implicit information in the text to create deeper meaning.

Seven Habits of Strong Readers	
Visualizing	Good readers make a movie in their heads while reading. Provide opportunities for students to sketch out, paint, or use descriptive words to create the setting and events in the texts you read with them. This may not come naturally to all learners, so teacher modeling will be important.
Monitor for Meaning	Teach students to pause throughout reading a text to think about and process what they have just read/heard you read. Allow them to clarify or re-tell what they've just heard to ensure that they're comprehending during pause points. The goal is for students to learn to do this independently.
Activate Prior Knowledge	Students will more readily grasp a concept if they have something to connect it to. Creating schema by building background knowledge allows a reader to understand the text more deeply, leading to increased fluency and comprehension.
Synthesize	Strong readers must connect the dots while reading. Teach them to look for information in multiple places in the text and use that textual evidence in their verbal or written responses. Even young learners can do this if it is modeled for them. Synthesizing also requires students to gather evidence throughout the text to create new meaning/understanding of character and theme.

Special Populations

We would be remiss to neglect discussing special populations in our classrooms and the scaffolding that can take place to help them access complex tasks. They are not exempt from rigorous activities. When provided with appropriate support, all students can and will be able to complete rigorous activities. Although there are many special groups, we will focus on two: students with special needs and English learners.

Students With Special Needs

Students with special needs do not necessarily have a lower level of intelligence. They are capable of rigorous work, but they need extra support. In addition to the general scaffolding strategies we have discussed, there are additional ways to help them learn.

Core Extensions

Core extensions are designed to extend the learning time of the core content by giving students more time to learn the core curriculum. This approach may allow the student more think time regarding the standard and, if taught correctly, provides the teacher and interventionist the time to enhance the lesson delivery to better meet the needs of the student. For example, use of visuals and concrete manipulative instruction is highly effective for low-performing students. However, these instructional tools require more time for implementation. A core extension allows for that time.

Preteaching

Another option within intervention is to preteach academic content. Many students who receive additional or clarifying instruction on a content may start to develop a dependency on that support. If they believe that they are less successful in the core classroom than they are during their support class, then they have the tendency to ignore core instruction and simply wait for the support class to explain what they didn't understand, or worse, didn't try to learn.

Preteaching is when the support or intervention class prepares the students for the upcoming core content instruction. By receiving scaffolding content, the student experiences much of the instruction that they will see in the core and can contribute more readily to the conversation in the core. For example, before reading *Oranges in No Man's Land* by Elizabeth Laird, it is imperative to build students' prior knowledge of what life is like for children growing up in war-torn countries. With this preparation, the students would enter the core instruction having already been exposed to the background content necessary to fully understand Laird's message. This may make them more confident with the materials and competent with the level of conversation, interpretation, and analysis required of them (Lalley & Miller, 2006). Such confidence and competence may eventually increase students' academic learning time and thus their performance. While there is some support for preteaching, there are also roadblocks. Much preparation must go into the content and instructional design so that the same approach is matched between the core and preteaching interventionist. For more information, see http://nycdoeit.airws.org/pdf/Preteaching.pdf.

Layering Meaning

A particular concern with older elementary students is when they cannot read grade-level text. Sometimes you must start with easier text in order to build to more complex text, which will deepen understanding. One strategy for supporting students who are not reading at grade level is "layering meaning." While this strategy can be used for any student, it is especially useful for students who cannot yet read the grade-level or assigned text material because it helps you find another text on the same topic that is written at an easier level. Students read that selection first to build their own knowledge and vocabulary; then they can go back and read the more complex text with your support. It's an excellent strategy, one that encourages rigor because students move beyond the easier text, but one that requires texts at differing levels. Technology is our solution. There are a variety of websites that provide leveled texts for your use.

Sources for Leveled Text

News in Levels (www.newsinlevels.com) and FortheTeachers (www.fortheteachers.org/reading_skills/) also provide varying levels of an article or text. FortheTeachers has science, health, and other topics, but information is language arts oriented.

Books That Grow (www.booksthatgrow.com) has a library of texts that have each been edited to be made accessible to different reading levels. There is a fee.

TweenTribune (http://tweentribune.com) is produced by the Smithsonian. It also provides an article at different levels but adds a quiz (moderately high-level questions) and allows teachers to create virtual classrooms to monitor progress and moderate comments.

Readworks (www.readworks.org) is a little different – they do texts, including paired texts, but they do *not* provide differing levels of the same text.

Text Compactor (www.textcompactor.com) lets you paste text into it and then automatically summarizes it (with a customized setting you control).

Rewordify (http://rewordify.com) allows a teacher or student to paste text into the screen, and it will identify challenging words and replace them with simpler ones or with explanations.

Freckle (freckle.com) provides an online reading platform, with a pre-assessment tool, that students can use to read texts at various levels.

Thanks to Larry Ferlazzo for these sources.

English Learners

English learners also have unique needs, some of which are met by the general scaffolding strategies we discussed. However, there are also more customized strategies that are helpful.

Technology

English language learners, for example, are often given simplified activities due to the language barrier. However, their lack of knowledge in speaking or writing English does not mean their growth in science, social studies, etc. should be stifled. Technology offers a wide array of constantly evolving tools to support students who learn differently. Discovery Education online allows students the opportunity to read, watch, and learn in their native language while they are learning English. Google Translate can take any text and convert it to one of 300 languages so that students can still access the content and learn at a high level. Likewise, students with a learning disability in writing can use Screencasting, Nearpod, or FlipGrid, which allows students to record themselves on any device, explaining their answer to a prompt or demonstrating their understanding of a text. Remember, the answers don't always have to come in the form of writing! Students who struggle with reading could use Microsoft Learning tools as a platform to break texts apart or have them read aloud to build fluency, confidence, and comprehension. Newsela and Freckle offer reading platforms that provide options for teachers to assign the same text with the same content but at various Lexile levels. All of these free tools will allow your special population to still have access to rigorous thinking and problem solving.

Visual Coding

Using color to deconstruct or draw attention to parts of a text can help English learners process information more effectively. This can be done by the teacher or by the student as you gradually release for independence. Perhaps when using a short story to highlight cause and effect, students can underline causes in green and effects in red. This could also work if you are teaching paragraph structure for an expository paragraph in your social studies lesson. If a teacher is consistent throughout the year with the same visual coding practices, students will recognize patterns more readily. For example, when showing examples of an expository paragraph, always highlight the topic sentence, circle transition words/phrases, number the evidence/reasons, and underline the concluding sentence. As students write their own paragraphs, have a peer use the same text markings to identify required structural elements for one another's writing. Finally, have students identify the elements in their own writing.

A K–2 classroom may use visual coding in a similar manner when identifying short story elements with directions on an anchor chart.

When You Find...	*Draw a...*
Setting	House
Character(s)	Stick figure
Events	Number them in order
Conflict	Frown
Solution	Smile

Three-Column Note-Taking

Oftentimes, students are simply asked to take notes, but they write down either everything in the text, or nothing. They do the same with teacher lectures. We've found that English learners take the best notes when they are provided with structure. Many teachers use a simple, two-column note-taking form. Key words are written in the left column. Using those as prompts, students take notes in the right column, with an appropriate numbering system provided so students know the exact amount of information to write. You can also add a third column, providing a place for students to draw an image that would remind them of the information. For K–2 students, you would simply use the columns in an anchor chart.

Sentence Frames

Sentence frames provide a basic structure for students. They are provided a "frame," which allows them to fill in key information. In many ways, it is a note-taking guide, but with more defined support. Students may complete it individually, but it is helpful if they can work with partners. This can be a way to scaffold the writing process for students.

English and Social Studies Sentence Frame Examples for Topic Sentences

In the early 1800s, ________________ provided many opportunities for growth.

There were many similarities and differences between the ________________ and ________________ in the sixteenth century.

In the beginning, Mrs. Luella Bates Washington Jones is very______________, but by the end of the story she learns becomes more ____________________.

In *Giraffe Problems*, Giraffe's main problem is __________________ ________________.

To simplify this for the younger student, consider creating sight word cards. Students can match the cards to create a sentence of their own, experimenting with syntax and logical order of words.

Other Strategies

There are a variety of other strategies you can use with your English learners. Remember to choose the one(s) that best meet your students' needs.

Other Strategies

- Provide opportunities to participate in small groups or work with a partner.
- Respect that they may need more reflection time, so you will need to provide more wait time.
- Allow some use of native language during scaffolding time.
- Be aware of cultural examples or vocabulary students may be unaware of.
- Use literature/examples in class that represent their culture.
- Incorporate realia whenever possible.

Conclusion

Supporting your students so they are able to access rigorous material and learn at high levels is crucial. The majority of your students will not intuitively or voluntarily think on a critical level unless you lead them to that point. This does not mean they are not capable. It simply means they need to be taught *how* to learn challenging material by providing them with tools to unlock meaning as well as receiving ongoing prompting to stimulate deeper thinking. As you increase the level of rigor for students, you will need to increase your support and scaffolding.

Points to Ponder

- The most important thing learned. . .
- One strategy I want to implement now
- One strategy I want to save for later. . .
- I'd like to learn more about. . .
- I'd like to share with other teachers. . .

5

Demonstration of Learning

In Chapter 3, we discussed rigorous expectations, including providing examples of rigorous tasks and assignments. In this chapter, we provide a variety of classroom approaches that allow students to demonstrate their understanding at a deep level.

Five Areas

1. Rigorous questioning strategies
2. Using writing to process learning
3. Academic discourse
4. Collaboration
5. Interactive experiences

Rigorous Questioning Strategies

Our questioning strategies reflect our high expectations. When we ask students higher-order questions, we are showing them we expect them to answer at higher levels. On the other hand, when we only ask students recall questions such as "Who did this?", we are demonstrating that we don't really expect them to know any more than the most basic answers. There are several general strategies you should incorporate as you question students.

General Questioning Strategies

- Provide adequate wait time.
- Call on a variety of students, not just those who raise their hands.
- Ask higher-order questions.
- If you ask a lower-level question, follow up with a higher-order question.
- Encourage follow-up questions from students.
- If a student struggles with the answer, provide guidance and scaffolding rather than moving to another student.

Types of Questioning

Next, we'll look at three models for rigorous questioning. Each provides insight into effective questioning. Choose or blend models to help you craft rigorous questioning for your lesson.

Three Questioning Models

1. Four categories
2. Transfer of learning
3. Essential questions

Four Categories

Another way to look at questioning is a set of four categories developed by James and Aschner (1963). These blend nicely with Webb's Depth of Knowledge levels that we discussed earlier.

Four Categories

1. Memory questions focus on identifying, naming, defining, designating, and responding with yes or no. Key words are who, what, where, when.
2. Convergent-thinking questions focus on explaining, stating relationships, comparing, and contrasting. Key words are why, how, in what way.
3. Divergent-thinking questions focus on predicting, hypothesizing, inferring, and reconstructing. Key words are imagine, suppose, predict, if . . . then. . ., how might, can you create, what are some possible consequences.
4. Evaluative-thinking questions focus on valuing, defending, judging, and justifying choices. Key words are defend, judge, justify, what do you think, what is your opinion.

Transfer of Learning

In their book *Tools for Teaching Conceptual Understanding*, Julie Stern and Krista Ferraro discuss transfer of learning. Based on earlier work by Perkins and Saloman, they focus specifically on students' transfer of learning. They distinguish the transfer as academic or real world and high road (more rigorous) or low road (less rigorous).

Stern and Ferraro's Transfer of Learning		
Transfer to Academic Learning	Low Road (less rigorous)	Transfer to highly similar school tasks
Transfer to Academic Learning	High Road (more rigorous)	Transfer to highly dissimilar school tasks
Transfer to Real-World Learning	Low Road (less rigorous)	Transfer to highly similar, real-world scenarios
Transfer to Real-World Learning	High Road (more rigorous)	Transfer to highly dissimilar, real-world scenarios (Innovation)

Let's look at how this works in the ELA and social studies classrooms.

English/Language Arts Examples		
Type of Transfer	*Low Road*	*High Road*
Academic	After characterizing Simba in the graveyard scene, how would you characterize him when he returns to Pride Rock?	How could you use characterization in your social studies class when learning about historical figures?
Real World	Use characterization to tell us about someone in your family. What does he/she do and say that reveals personality? What do others say about him/her? What would you tell us about this person?	If we learn about characters through their appearance, words, actions, and what others say about them, how can we use characterization to help us to make wise choices of friends?

Social Studies Examples		
Type of Transfer	*Low Road*	*High Road*
Academic	We've been studying landforms in social studies. Where can we find these landforms in our country?	How might these landforms impact the economy of the area?
Real World	Identify five examples of how goods and services impact you.	If you could create an empire of your own, how would you regulate the exchange of goods and services? Explain your rationale.

Essential Questions

Another way to look at questioning is through the seven defining characteristics of essential questions. McTighe and Wiggins (2013) explain the

> "aim is to stimulate thought, to provoke inquiry, and to spark more questions including thoughtful student questions, not just page answers. They are provocative and generative. By tackling such questions, learners are engaged in uncovering the depth and richness of a topic that might otherwise be obscured by simply covering it" (p. 3).

Seven Defining Characteristics of an Essential Question

1 Is open-ended
2. Is thought-provoking and intellectually engaging
3. Calls for higher-order thinking
4. Points toward important, transferable ideas
5. Raises additional questions
6. Requires support and justification
7. Recurs over time

Based on the essential elements, they provide a questioning framework that can be used for ELA and social studies.

Questioning Framework		
Facet	*ELA Sample Question*	*Social Studies Sample Question*
Explanation	What is plot structure?	What is the Prime Meridian?
Interpretation	How does Willy Wonka's use of humor make a difference for Charlie and his grandfather?	How do latitude and longitude affect climate?
Application	How might you use onomatopoeia in your own writing?	Why is it important to learn about food safety issues around the world?
Perspective	How might *The Rough-Face Girl* be different if written from the cruel sister's perspective?	How might the phrase "freedom for all" be interpreted differently by various countries?
Empathy	What did Elenor Coerr intend to make us feel about Sadako in *Sadako and The Thousand Paper Cranes*?	What feelings and emotions did you experience as you've learned about the struggle of Japanese families during World War II?
Self-Knowledge	How can I best make meaning of a poem?	How does my cultural background shape the way I interact with others?

Using Technology in Questioning

Many apps exist today to integrate technology with questioning. This engages students and allows them to answer safely, all at once, and you decide which answers to display and further discuss. Some students will be more comfortable responding in this format, and you get an instant snapshot of everyone's thoughts on the question you pose.

Apps to Use With Questioning

Animoto – Gives students the ability to make a short, 30-second share video of what they learned in a given lesson

AnswerGarden – A tool for online brainstorming or polling, educators can use this real-time tool to see student feedback on questions

Answer Pad – A graphical student response system with the ability to poll and leave feedback. The blank pad functions like an individual whiteboard for each student.

AudioNote – A combination of a voice recorder and notepad that captures both audio and notes for student collaboration

Dotstorming – A whiteboard app that allows digital sticky notes to be posted and voted on. This tool is best for generating class discussion and brainstorming on different topics and questions.

Obsurvey – Create surveys, polls, and questionnaires quickly and easily

PollDaddy – Quick and easy way to create online polls, quizzes, and questions. Students can use smartphones, tablets, and computers to provide their answers, and information can be culled for reports.

Poll Everywhere – Teachers can create a feedback poll or ask questions. Students respond in various ways, and teachers see the results in real time. With open-ended questions, you can capture data and spin up tag clouds to aggregate response. There is a limit to the number of users.

The Queue – Free educational chat tool that mirrors Twitter and allows teachers to post questions and students to respond via the thread. Students can respond via text or video, and the tool allows "journeys" in which teachers introduce a topic via video and connect students to participating resources. Great for gathering formative assessment data at the beginning, middle or end of units.

Source: www.nwea.org/blog/2018/the-ultimate-list-65-digital-tools-and-apps-to-support-formative-assessment-practices/

Using Writing to Process Learning

It is a common practice to use writing to assess knowledge acquired, but what about allowing students to process information through writing? Traditional writing instruction has changed over the past two decades as millennials and now postmillennials fill our classrooms. Let's look at how the traditional approach differs from today's best pedagogical practices.

Traditional Approaches Versus the Process/Workshop Approach	
Traditional Approaches to Teaching Writing	*Process/Workshop Approach to Teaching Writing*
Writing is a product to be evaluated.	Writing is a process to be experienced and, whenever possible, shared.
There is one correct procedure for writing.	There are many processes for different situations, subjects, audiences, and authors.
Writing is taught rather than learned through experience.	The writing experience is coached and predominantly learned through guided practice and shared experience.
The process of writing is essentially linear: planning precedes writing and revisions follows drafting, etc.	Writing processes are varied and recursive. One might start at different points in the process.
Writers must be taught in small, incremental parts. That is, small parts and subskills must be mastered before attempting whole pieces of writing.	Writers learn best from attempting whole texts and learning about the parts of those texts while in the recursive process of writing/revising/writing, etc.
Writing can be done swiftly and on command.	The rhythms and pace of writing can be quite slow, since the writer's actual task is to create meaning.
Writing is a silent and solitary activity.	Writing is essentially social and collaborative.

Source: http://www3.canisius.edu/~justice/CSTmodule-final/CSTmodule-final17.html#headingtaglink_3

Originally adapted from Emig (1982), in Zemmelman, S., & Daniels, H. (1988). *A community of writers*. Portsmouth, NH: Heinemann.

Notice the process approach centers around not only the writing process but thinking as a reflective process. There are a variety of ways to incorporate a process-based focus in your classroom. We will look at two: Writer's Workshop and Document-Based Questioning, each of which can be used in both English/language arts and social studies classrooms.

Writer's Workshop

Writer's Workshop revolves around certain criteria that primarily include mini-lessons, work time, conferencing, and publishing. Growth in knowledge can happen for many students in giving them time and space to write about what they are learning, whether in ELA or social studies or any other class. Teachers can learn a great deal about seeing a student's evolution of thoughts over time, and this can happen in a workshop environment in which students feel less threatened or constrained by time. This takes time. A true writer's workshop, as outlined by Nancy Atwell in her book *In the Middle*, calls for student choice in topic and genre. This is certainly necessary at times; however, we all know that standards call for us to ensure that specific writing modes must be taught and addressed. What if we allowed students to choose a topic within certain parameters and then used elements from the workshop approach? See the table for two examples that allow you to explicitly teach writing as students have an opportunity to process their learning over a period of several days. Note that the mini-lesson, writing time, conferencing, and editing will cycle through for multiple days before publishing.

English/Language Arts	*Social Studies*
Assignment: Choose any character from our short story unit and re-tell it as a poem. Be sure to use textual evidence and convey the same tone and central message in your new piece. Mini-lesson ideas: ♦ Discuss tone and central message of a story ♦ Brainstorming ideas for topics ♦ Free verse vs. narrative poems	Assignment: Write a letter to a pen pal from a different country and consider how you might express the important values and ideas of your culture and/or family traditions. Mini-lesson ideas: ♦ Understanding the structure of a friendly letter ♦ Exploring cultural identity ♦ Brainstorming family traditions

English/Language Arts	*Social Studies*
♦ Organizing ideas . . . which events/ideas will you be sure to include in your poem ♦ Punctuation in poetry ♦ Using word choice to establish tone Writing time: This follows a 10- to 15-minute mini-lesson and allows students to immediately practice what you've modeled with their own writing.	♦ Establishing voice and audience ♦ Organizing ideas ♦ Using specific ideas vs. general ♦ Including appropriate punctuation
Conferencing: Hold 2- to 3-minute conferences with each student to touch base on their writing. You may not get to every student each day, but be sure to take note of what you discuss and give each student specific praise and a specific goal. Allow opportunities for peer conferencing as well. Publishing: After several days of student monitoring progress through workshop time, give students a deadline for publishing their work in the format you desire.	Writing time: This follows a 10- to 15-minute mini-lesson and allows students to immediately practice what you've modeled with their own writing. Conferencing: Hold 2- to 3-minute conferences with each student to touch base on their writing. You may not get to every student each day, but be sure to take note of what you discuss and give each student specific praise and a specific goal. Allow opportunities for peer conferencing as well. Publishing: After several days of student monitoring progress through workshop time, give students a deadline for publishing their work in the format you desire.

Using a workshop approach to writing in your classes can be an occasional technique in which you give students a "time out" from receiving new content and allow them to process what they are learning through writing. Writer's Workshop takes time. It is not something you would necessarily want to do every week or even every month. However, when used intentionally and purposefully, one week dedicated to showing students the value in taking time to develop thoughts can be much more effective than assigning multiple writing tasks with little instruction or feedback along the way. When you coach students through the process effectively, students typically produce higher-quality writing and begin to think of themselves as writers. This can happen with effective conferencing, both teacher–student conferencing and peer conferences.

It is important to note that simply requiring students to revise and edit their work before turning it in has value as a metacognitive process in itself. When necessary, this can be accomplished without implementing a formal, lengthy Writer's Workshop. For example, before tenth grade history students submit a response to an essay you've assigned, conduct a mini-lesson on in-text citations and ask them to revise their work to include their sources within the text. Or perhaps you've noticed that students aren't utilizing commentary to support their evidence, so you pull some examples and explicitly show them how to expand on their facts by making connections and/or elaborating. You could do a short lesson on any skill or area in which you notice common errors and have students revise their work with intense focus on that skill before turning in their assignment. Utilize the elements of Writer's Workshop as you see fit in your classroom to help students take their writing to a deeper level as they use it to process the knowledge they're acquiring.

Don't shy away from writer's workshop in grades K–2. Students can absolutely still learn the writing process and develop writing techniques early on, but you will need to rely on drawing and telling strategies. The following apps are great ideas for implementing a workshop approach with emergent writers.

Apps for Younger Learners	
Draw and Tell (by Duck Duck Moose)	Young learners can draw their story and tell about it through voice recording.
Easy Stop Motion Studio ($3.99)	Students create cartoon characters and settings from scratch using shape templates, and then set them into motion as they tell their story.
Superhero Comic Book Maker	Create personalized animated comic strips to tell an original story!
Toontastic 3D	Students can make their imagination come to life by drawing characters and bringing them to life through 3D settings. This app uses a microphone to record characters' voices.
Chatterpix	Students can take a picture of anything, draw a line for an animated mouth, add accessories, and record their voice to bring the picture to life.

Mini-Q's

Another way for students to process learning through writing is Document-Based Questioning (DBQ), which has become popular in recent years. DBQ prompts students to answer a question that requires them to state a claim and support it with evidence, analysis, and reasoning. DBQ thinking does not have to be reserved for middle and high school students. DBQ Project researchers observed numerous classrooms from kindergarten through fifth grade and found that young school children are capable of evidence-based thinking and writing (www.dbqproject.com/). Based on this, The DBQ Project developed a concept referred to as Mini-Q's, which offer primary source documents, background texts, and a controlling question for elementary students. More commonly used in social studies classrooms, Mini-Q's are also useful in language arts classrooms. In our language arts classrooms, we found that students would simply look for events that occurred during a piece of literature to answer a question. In a Mini-Q, students need to make an argument by moving beyond summarizing events to deeper analysis of the text.

Mini-Q's are designed to require students to demonstrate their learning at a high level. As we explored the concept of Mini-Q's in more detail, we found there are four areas in which this educational tool can be rigorous for students.

Using Document-Based Questions, Students Will. . .

1. Analyze sources for observations vs. inferences
2. Draw conclusions with the aid of the documents provided
3. Make connections between the documents
4. Bring in outside knowledge to justify overall learning

Four Key Components

There are four key components of DBQ: the question, supporting texts and documents, the instruction that provides students scaffolding to be successful, and the assessment criteria. First, Document-Based Questions are designed to require students to make an argument, supporting it with evidence and justification.

Sample ELA Document-Based Question	*Sample Social Studies Document-Based Question*
Question: How did the Civil War, increased number of immigrants, and the economy of our country impact children of the late 1800s and early 1900s?	Question: Why did the colonies almost fail to thrive?
Documents/Texts:	Documents/Texts:
The Boxcar Children books	Topographical map of the original thirteen colonies
Historical photos from early 1900s of orphan trains	Original letter (read aloud by teacher) from a colonist about the conditions
Nonfiction picture books about orphan trains	Historical record of climate/weather along the Eastern coast
Diary entry of an orphan who experienced the orphan train	Picture books on the colonies

Next, students work with a variety of documents to respond to the questions.

Sample Document Types for ELA Classrooms	*Sample Document Types for Social Studies Classrooms*
Excerpts from texts	Primary source documents
Short stories	Excerpts from texts
Poems	News articles (Scholastic Kids is great)
Diary entries	Political cartoons (age appropriate)
Artwork Photographs	

Third, students need appropriate instruction to support the process. This may occur during whole-class instruction or small group coaching and during full lessons or mini-lessons. In order for students to work at rigorous levels, such as providing justification for conclusions and going beyond the text to make connections, you can provide mini-lessons on key strategies.

Sample Mini-Lessons to Support DBQ

- ♦ Making observations vs. making inferences
- ♦ Distinguishing between fact and opinion
- ♦ Using outside knowledge to draw conclusions
- ♦ Identifying primary vs. secondary source material

Regardless of age or reading level, using documents to support and enrich learning in your classroom is beneficial; in fact, they will help students gain deeper access to texts that may be too difficult to understand in isolation. Coupled with rich classroom discussion, this level of engagement will increase the rigor in your classroom.

Rigorous Conversations: Academic Discourse

When we think about traditional student talk, whether it is in response to a teacher's question, discussion with other students, or generating questions, there are common problems.

Problems With Student Talk in the Classroom

- Controlled by teacher
- Too little student talk
- Too focused on simply answering teacher's questions
- Surface level rather than in depth
- Dominated by a few students, typically excluding struggling students

In recent years, the conversation has shifted from classroom talk and discussion to student discourse. What exactly is the difference? Student discourse is focused on "on-task" talk, as well as the use of academic vocabulary. In other words, not only is discourse more rigorous, it is more purposeful.

Discourse With a PURPOSE

Promotes critical thinking
Understanding at a deep level is desired result
Reflection is encouraged
Partners, groups, and individuals use academic vocabulary
Ownership by students
Specific classroom norms enable discourse
Each student participates

Promotes Critical Thinking

Simple, low-level conversations should be, at best, a minor part of your classroom. Although there is a time and place for basic information, it should always lead to higher-level, critical thinking.

Sample Prompting Tasks to Facilitate Academic Conversation and Critical Thinking		
	Low Level	*Critical Thinking*
English/Language Arts	Provide students with sentences in which they must determine what punctuation to use to make it a complete sentence. (With this prompt, students aren't making decisions together or considering effect of the punctuation.)	Provide students with sentences of varied length and structure. Ask them to discuss how the punctuation used in each changes the pace, tone, and flow of the sentence. Require them to determine how the punctuation can be changed to achieve a different tone or pace.
Social Studies	Ask students to work as a group to research a topic. (With this prompt, students could, in theory, simply divide the topics and research in isolation.)	In your groups, determine the best strategy for researching your assigned topic, who is best suited to research each topic, and how to organize your information to teach peers.

Understanding at a Deep Level Is Desired Result

Similar to promoting critical thinking, discourse results in deeper understanding.

Examples of Discourse That Lead to Deeper Understanding	
English/Language Arts	*Social Studies*
Discussion of characters' motives and/or choices Discussion of why an author made certain decisions in his/her writing Discussion of use of conventions in writing Analysis of a text	Discussion of possible research questions Developing a hypothesis or speculating about a solution Thorough discussion of the impact of a historical event or invention

Reflection Is Encouraged

Reflection should be an ongoing part of discourse. Students should self-reflect, which then results in partner or group reflection. Students may need starter prompts to guide the reflective process.

Sample Reflection Prompts

- How did you decide. . . ?
- What would happen if. . . ?
- Have you considered. . . ?
- What would you suggest for. . . ?
- How might an author. . . ?
- What was your intention when. . . ?
- What is the connection between _____ and _____?
- How would an anthropologist. . . ?

Partners, Groups, and Individuals Use Academic Vocabulary

A key distinguishing mark of discourse is the use of academic language. You'll want to incorporate academic vocabulary throughout your instruction and model its use so students will use it in their discussions.

Sample Academic Vocabulary	
English/Language Arts	*Social Studies*
Textual evidence	Latitude/longitude
Word choice	Goods/services
Fact/opinion	Culture
Fiction/nonfiction	Artifact
Biography/autobiography	Historical
Analyze	Similarities/differences
Visualize	Globe
Character	Continent
Conflict	Justify
Plot	Label
Setting	Issue
Narrative	Locate
Compare/contrast	Primary vs. secondary
Predict	
Synonym/antonym	

Ownership by Students

We discussed the importance of developing student ownership in Chapter 2, but we'd like to reinforce that in this context. Academic discourse is more effective when students share ownership. You can facilitate ownership by providing choices in what and how they discuss content or giving them a voice in the development of the structure of groups. For example, you may allow students to choose their groups, although you need to be careful about students excluding others or cliques that may develop. You might also introduce the lesson and allow students to decide appropriate times to work in pairs or small groups. This is a common activity, but for us to provide a more rigorous experience, we must focus on what students are doing to encourage higher-order thinking from one another.

Specific Classroom Norms Enable Discourse

If we want to incorporate discourse into our classroom, we cannot assume that it will automatically occur. In addition to teaching students what to discuss, we need to provide and teach a set of norms explaining how to discuss.

Sample Classroom Norms for Discourse

- We are all a team, so we work together rather than competing.
- We respect each other and act appropriately.
- We actively listen to each other, which allows us to authentically contribute our perspectives.
- If you don't agree with someone, find a positive way to respond without embarrassing the other person.
- Everyone should be able to participate. If one person is talking too much, the other group members should give them a signal and move on.
- The process is just as important as the result. We want to think deeply about our work, elaborate, justify our points, and pose additional questions to promote more thinking.
- If you need help, check out the Resource Board for questioning prompts and/or sample vocabulary.

Each Student Participates

As we said earlier, a challenge you likely face is when a few students dominate discussions, whether it is in the whole class or in small groups or pairs. When you are guiding a whole-class discussion, you can minimize this by calling on a variety of students, regardless of who raises their hands. You can also provide an opportunity to share with a partner before you ask for answers as a whole group, which encourages participation. In small groups, if you have issues with particular students and an individual conversation does not take care of the issue, you might consider using a timer or a timekeeper to limit the amount of time each student can speak or using tokens to be used for each comment. When a student runs out of tokens, they are no longer allowed to speak. Although neither of these is ideal because they inhibit conversation, it may be necessary to ensure all students can participate. A related challenge to participation is when students get stuck or don't know what to say, and therefore, they don't say anything. In this case, we want to encourage students, which we can do by providing question starters. The goal is for other students to ask the starter questions so that the group can continue its discussion.

Starter Questions

To Prompt More Thinking:

- You are on the right track. Tell us more.
- You are onto something. Keep going.
- The teacher said there is no right answer, so what would be your best answer?

To Fortify or Justify a Response:

- What is your opinion about. . . ?
- Why is what you said important?
- Explain how you got that answer.

To See Others' Points of View:

- How is your process different from mine?
- Do you see another way we could come up with a solution?

To Consider Consequences:

- How can we apply this to real life?
- What did you learn in another lesson that we can connect this to?
- How else can we use this?

Source: Adapted from: http://ptgmedia.pearsoncmg.com/images/9780205627585/downloads/Echevarria_math_Ch1_TheAcademicLanguageofMathematics.pdf

Using Collaboration to Increase Rigor

There is a wide range of classroom activities in which students collaborate to process learning and demonstrate understanding. For example,

Student Cooperative Learning Rubric

	You're a Team Player **3**	You're Working on It. . . **2**	You're the Lone Ranger **1**	Total for Each Category
G **Group Dedication**	I listened respectfully to my teammates' ideas and offered suggestions that helped my group.	I did listen to ideas, but I didn't give suggestions.	I was distracted and more interested in the other groups than my group.	Group Dedication I circled number 3 2 1
R **Responsibility**	I eagerly accepted responsibility with my group and tried to do my part to help everyone in my group.	I accepted responsibility within my group without arguing.	I quarreled and did not accept roles given by my group.	Responsibility I circled number 3 2 1
O **Open Communication**	I listened to others' ideas and tried to solve conflicts peacefully.	I listened to others' ideas, but did not try to solve conflicts.	I was controlling and argumentative to my group.	Open Communication I circled number 3 2 1
U **Use of Work Time**	I was involved and engaged. I encouraged my group the entire time we were working.	I tried my best the entire time we were working.	I was not involved and did not offer any suggestions for the good of the group.	Use of Work Time I circled number 3 2 1
P **Participation**	I was a team member. I offered ideas, suggestions, and help for my group.	I participated in the project, but did not offer to help anyone.	I did not participate because I was not interested.	Participation I circled number 3 2 1
				Total ___________

Source: Reproduced with permission from Blackburn and Witzel, *Rigor for Students with Special Needs*.

students typically work together for project- and problem-based learning and Genius Hour, all of which we discussed in Chapter 3. Here, we'll look at two other specific options: jigsaw/expert groups and literature circles. Following is a rubric for student collaboration, no matter what type of cooperative learning you are doing in the classroom.

Jigsaw/Expert Groups

Rather than being the sole holder of knowledge in your classroom, use expert groups followed by the jigsaw method of group work. Students are assigned to small groups (groups of four are ideal). Next, students number themselves in the groups. Each student will become an expert on a particular topic. All students who are numbered one move together to study their assigned area. Students who are number two do the same, as do numbers three and four. A key part of working in the larger groups is that members agree on the most important aspects of their topic. Third, the "experts" return to their original groups of four students. In turn, each expert teaches his or her subject to his or her small group. Finally, the teacher leads a whole-group discussion of the topics.

You can use this any time you would like to have students teach each other. For example, a teacher could split up a chapter in the book for each of the expert groups to create a rap to teach their smaller groups. Not only would this be engaging, students would be required to use higher-order skills to create a rap that represented the content. As another alternative, you can also have "expert" groups create multimedia presentations that can be shared with their individual groups.

Jigsaw in Ten Easy Steps

1. Divide students into five- or six-person jigsaw groups. The groups should be diverse in terms of gender, ethnicity, race, and ability.
2. Appoint one student from each group as the leader. Initially, this person should be the most mature student in the group.
3. Divide the day's lesson into five or six segments. For example, if you want history students to learn about Eleanor Roosevelt, you might divide a short biography of her into stand-alone segments on: (1) her childhood, (2) her family life with Franklin and their children, (3) her life after Franklin contracted polio, (4) her work in the White House as First Lady, and (5) her life and work after Franklin's death.
4. Assign each student to learn one segment, making sure students have direct access only to their own segment.
5. Give students time to read over their segment at least twice and become familiar with it. There is no need for them to memorize it.
6. Form temporary "expert groups" by having one student from each jigsaw group join other students assigned to the same segment. Give students in these expert groups time to discuss the main points of their segment and to rehearse the presentations they will make to their jigsaw group.
7. Bring the students back into their jigsaw groups.
8. Ask each student to present her or his segment to the group. Encourage others in the group to ask questions for clarification.
9. Float from group to group, observing the process. If any group is having trouble (e.g., a member is dominating or disruptive), make an appropriate intervention. Eventually, it's best for the group leader to handle this task. Leaders can be trained by whispering an instruction on how to intervene until the leader gets the hang of it.
10. At the end of the session, give a quiz on the material so that students quickly come to realize that these sessions are not just fun and games but really count.

Source: www.jigsaw.org/steps.htm

Literature Circles

Literature circles offer an opportunity for students to collaborate with one another in a smaller, well-structured environment. Don't assume because the word "literature" is in the title that this is only an English/

language arts strategy. This approach is effective with a wide range of texts, including primary source documents. And even if students are not reading independently yet, literature circles can be completed using audio books as students follow along.

With a piece of text as the focal point for learning, three to five group members each take on a different role, which sets the purpose for their reading. This role determines the perspective from which they will read the text and how they will want to process the text. Students come to the circle to discuss their ideas and impressions of the assigned reading and, through academic discourse, share thoughts with one another. With this small-group format, students feel less vulnerable than when participating in a whole-class discussion. The conversations become more authentic and intimate as the group develops trust and respect for one another's ideas. Melissa has often had students reflect that literature circles helped them appreciate their classmates' different points of view and allowed them to focus intently on one aspect of the reading instead of trying to remember everything. One particular student commented that relying on a group to help her make meaning of the text from different angles really helped her understand that reading doesn't have to be a chore done in isolation; rather, it is much better when it is viewed as an activity that can be shared with others.

Literature circles can be used with novels, short stories, essays, poems, or informative texts, or primary source documents in the social studies classroom. They can take place intermittently over the course of a unit or be completed in a single day with a shorter text. The concepts remain the same: students working together to approach a text from various perspectives in order to gain a deeper understanding. The only things you'll need to adapt are the roles students will complete. These are dependent on what you would like for them to get from the text and how you would like for them to process the text. The following charts provide examples of role sets that could be used with students. Expanded descriptions of the roles are provided in the eResources at www.routledge.com/9781138598959.

English/Language Arts: Novel or Short Story	
Role	*Description*
Discussion Leader	Develop X questions (with answers). Lead a discussion in your group.
Artist	Draw a picture that relates to the text and explain its significance.
Word Wizard	Find words/phrases that are difficult to understand. Look up their meanings and teach them to your peers.
Bridge Builder	Make connections! Text to text, text to self, or text to world . . . and share them with your peers.

Social Studies: Informative Text	
Role	*Description*
Discussion Leader	Develop X questions (with answers and page references) at different levels. Lead discussion.
Time Traveler	Make a timeline of important events in the text. How did one event lead to the next?
Word Wizard	Note the academic terminology used in the text. Look into what these mean more deeply and teach them to your peers.
Bridge Builder	Make connections between the text we have read today and what we have discussed in class. You will also need to make connections to how this relates to our previous unit in history and how it impacts the world we live in today.

On the day of a scheduled literature circle meeting, students should come prepared with their assigned role sheet completed. In no particular order, each will share what they noticed in the text and how their thoughts evolved when reading through the particular lens of their assigned task. To help students be active listeners, you may consider having them take minutes from their meeting. This serves as a record of what was discussed and what ideas were fleshed out during their time together, but it also provides accountability for participation in the literature circle meeting. An example of how you might ask them to listen and process the information and ideas their peers share is available online with the eResources at www.routledge.com/9781138598959. This would be adapted depending on the roles used in your literature circle.

Together, students will make much deeper meaning of a text than if they simply read it alone and answer comprehension questions. As students work together, you may also take advantage of technology tools to support their collaboration.

Sample Technology Tools to Support Collaboration	
Backchannel Chat **Price**: $15/year/class; $299/year/school **Platforms**: Android, Chrome, iOS, and web **Grades**: 7–12	Backchannel Chat's moderated online discussions are intended to engage students and encourage them to share. Think of it as a teacher-moderated, private version of Twitter, where students can discuss topics that might just transcend the virtual space. Setup is quick and easy: teachers sign up, name their chat, and give students the URL. Students can join with only a name; no other personal information is required. Teachers can moderate discussions, remove messages, and "lock" the chat at any time.
NowComment **Price**: Free **Platforms**: Web **Grades**: K–12	NowComment is a document annotation and discussion platform that allows students to mark up and discuss texts. Upload a document (in any number of formats) to create an online discussion area. Paragraphs for text are numbered, with the document shown on the left and the comment panel on the right. You can control when students can comment on a document and when they can see each other's comments. For group projects or peer-reviewed activities, you can have students upload their own documents.
Mindmeister **Price**: Free **Platforms**: Web **Grades**: K–8	This platform allows students to collaborate in planning for/designing a story, essay, presentation, etc. Much like a Google Doc, students can work on it simultaneously, expanding on one another's thoughts as they work.

Source: Excerpted from: www.commonsense.org/education/blog/5-online-discussion-tools-to-fuel-student-engagement

Creating Interactive Experiences to Deepen Learning

By actually experiencing an event or situation, students can take a one-dimensional concept and turn it in to simulated reality, which provides for more rigorous learning. Let's look at two examples.

I Think/You Think

One activity that allows students to actively participate in their learning in grades 3–5 is I Think/You Think. Students must research a topic thoroughly enough to be able to anticipate and refute an argument in an instant. Lindsay Yearta uses an early form of debate to teach her students to see different perspectives on an issue. She begins with a handout that includes a statement: "I am for/against (insert your topic here)." Next, she assigns each student a position (for or against). The students circle their position on a handout and then research three reasons to support their position. She says,

> They get into their groups and come up with what they think the other group would say. What do you think their points are going to be? Then, they write down at least three points their opposition might have and they research comebacks to the opposition's points. So, they have to think ahead and research not only their position, but the other side as well. Then, when we hold our debate, each student had to speak at least once.

The verbal exchange is supported by the depth of research on both points of view. To increase rigor, students must support and justify their claims with research, testimonials, textual evidence, etc. Note: Many of these debates can actually be turned into seminar discussions as well to make them feel less threatening, but more thought-provoking.

If you would like more ideas on holding various kinds of debates in your elementary classroom, visit www.educationworld.com and search for debates in primary class.

Sample Debate Topics	
English/Language Arts	*Social Studies*
In *From the Elephant Pit,* was the hunter better off because he rescued the man from the pit?	Should recycling be mandatory?
The internet should be banned from schools.	Should our students wear school uniforms?
Teachers should be replaced with online learning.	All American citizens should be required to vote.
After reading *The One and Only Ivan,* do you think zoos should be banned?	Should children be limited to two hours of screen time per day?
In *The Giving Tree,* should the tree have given all of herself away?	Should gum be allowed in class?

Virtual Reality

In today's technological world, we would be remiss to not mention the opportunity that the growing field of virtual reality offers. Take your students beyond the text by integrating VR into your classroom. Monica Burns, founder of ClassTechTips and EdTech consultant, suggests that even without a class set of Google Cardboards or other VR devices, you can still incorporate virtual reality into your curriculum and help students experience facets of an otherwise one-dimensional text. Instead of simply reading about the seven continents, use an interactive whiteboard or iPads and allow them to see and "experience" the sights and sounds of the various continents. Allow your students the opportunity to accompany two Himalayan schoolgirls on their daily six-hour trek to school or take a 360-degree tour of the Sphinx and pyramids at Giza. In English/language arts classes, virtually take your students to Southeast Asia to show them the setting of *Wing's Visit to Singapore* or provide an opportunity for them to climb to base camp on Mt. Everest when reading the novel *Everest On Top of the World.* Before reading a biography on Nelson Mandela, take a virtual field trip to visit the slums of Johannesburg, South Africa, to get a glimpse of the cause for which he fought. The options are endless, so take advantage of all the free material online to transform learning as your students know it.

Sources for Virtual-Reality Education

National Geographic's YouTube Channel

A series of 360° videos captures virtual reality from any web browser and touch-screen device.

Nearpod.com

Excellent VR lessons for students of all ages across all content.

Discovery Ed

Hundreds of videos that transport students to locations around the world in an instant.

BBC 360° (YouTube)

Allows students to experience the sights and sounds of destinations across the globe.

Google Arts and Culture (https://artsandculture.google.com/explore)

Takes people inside cultural and historical events and provides street views of famous landmarks or sites.

Conclusion

One facet of rigor is that students demonstrate learning at high levels. When you ask rigorous questions, utilize writing as a means of processing information, require the use of academic discourse in discussions, offer opportunities for collaboration and shared learning experiences, and integrate interactive experiences into your curriculum, you will see students move beyond providing basic information and begin showing their understanding at deeper levels.

Points to Ponder

- The most important thing learned...
- One strategy I want to implement now...
- One strategy I want to save for later...
- I'd like to learn more about...
- I'd like to share with other teachers...

6

Assessment

Assessment is a critical aspect of rigorous language arts and social studies classrooms. In this chapter, we'll look at the aspects of effective formative and summative assessments.

Effective Formative Assessment

Formative assessments, which are typically informal, take place throughout the instructional process. They should be administered frequently since they provide an immediate assessment of students' levels of mastery.

Dr. Gregory Firm, a former school superintendent, uses the term "informative assessment" because formative assessments are used to inform the teacher and the student of mastery and progress. He describes six characteristics of effective formative assessment. Although he discusses these characteristics related to math, we find them useful for all subject areas.

Effective Formative Assessment

1. Develop a meaningful feedback loop – provide ongoing feedback (data) to drive teacher and student actions.
2. Real-time feedback – formative feedback during the learning process so students will not continuously practice skills incorrectly
3. Independent learning – students learn to self-reflect, self-assess independently with limited guidance from the teacher. Independent learning is to be blended with teacher-led instruction to include online instruction such as "flipped classrooms."
4. Personalized learning – instruction and assessment are built around students' individual needs (student-centric teaching).
5. Active learning – continuous, dynamic, and adaptive so that it can capture where the child is on the landscape of learning – where they have been, what their struggles are and where they are going next.
6. Collaborative implementation – all stakeholders (district personnel, administrators, teachers) take part in the process of formative assessment.

Source: www.dreambox.com/blog/what-is-math-formative-assessment

Examples of Rigorous Formative Assessments

Let's look at formative assessments that can be used before, during, and after instruction. Then, we'll finish with technology options that can support your efforts.

Before Instruction

Entrance Slips

It is often critical to assess where your students are before even beginning a new lesson or unit. Prior to learning about George Washington, you may hand each of your students a sticky note as they come into class that day and ask them to write down what they already know (or what they think they know) about him. Or, in a language arts classroom, prior to a lesson on writing narratives, you ask them to write down what they think makes a good story. Each student brings their sticky note up and places it in the K column of a KWL chart. Then you can scan and group those notes quickly to discover facts they know and misconceptions they have and gauge what they don't know. This chart can be revisited after the lesson to see what students have learned.

Understanding Goals for Learning

Often, we state the standard, objective, or learning goal for students and then move into the lesson. In order to assess student understanding, ask students to reword the standard into a question they should be able to answer at the end of the lesson. Identifying and addressing whether students understand the standard itself will help facilitate understanding during the remainder of the lesson.

Observations

An important formative assessment tool for teachers is the use of observations. Observations can be planned, or they can be spontaneous. In an observation, you simply observe what students are doing, and take notes for documentation. You may choose to observe for particular instructional behaviors, or you may simply observe to see what happens from a general standpoint. Checklists, which provide a quick way for you to make notes about your observations, can be simple yes/no tallies, or they can be open ended for teachers to add notes.

Sample Language Arts Checklist

Characteristic	*Notes*
Student demonstrates ability to write a narrative paragraph.	
Student demonstrates persistence while writing.	
Student reflects on his/her writing and makes revisions throughout the process.	
Student shows applications of simple conventions (capital letters, punctuation).	

Time Management Tip

Definitely use a checklist when observing students. If it helps, use a grid, so you can put your criteria in the rows, and students' names in the columns. This will save time and focus your observation.

Interviews and Conferences

In interviews and conferences, the teacher meets with students to assess understanding of content, either before a lesson to gauge base knowledge or during a lesson for ongoing assessment. For either of these strategies, the teacher plans a series of questions to ask a student about his or her learning. It's also important to stay flexible, and adjust questions during the interview or conference. These are probably used most often in writing situations, but they can be used with any subject area.

Sample Conference Questions

Please tell me a little about your work.
What do you think is going well?
What are you struggling with?
Show me an example.
How do you think you can improve on your own?
How can I help you?
What are your next steps?

Anticipation Guides

Anticipation guides can be used to activate prior knowledge of your students, but they also allow insight into student thinking prior to a new text or topic. More thematic in nature, students in a third grade unit on heroes could benefit from gathering their own thoughts on the concepts before instruction begins. Again, it's interesting and formative to understand from which perspectives students are coming so that you can be sensitive to their backgrounds, their paradigms, and any misconceptions that are present.

Sample Anticipation Guide

Name: ______________________ Block: _________ Date: ___________

HERO ANTICIPATION GUIDE

Directions: Please complete the following chart according to your opinions. You will not be graded on your opinions. There is not necessarily one right answer, so answer honestly.

Agree	Disagree	Statement
_______	_______	1. Heroes are always courageous.
_______	_______	2. Courage always involves sacrifice.
_______	_______	3. There are many acts of courage in a war.
_______	_______	4. A hero is born that way and shows heroism through his or her actions.
_______	_______	5. A hero is always honest and law-abiding.
_______	_______	6. Someone can be considered a hero only if they win.
_______	_______	7. If a person does something heroic but gets something out of doing it, then she or he is not a hero.
_______	_______	8. A hero is someone who is different than the rest of society.
_______	_______	9. A hero's actions result in the greater good.

Source: Adapted from SpringBoard Curriculum

An example of a K–2 anticipation guide in a social studies lesson may include the use of smiles or frowns, checks or minuses, etc.

Put a check if you think the picture could represent the term hero.	Put a check if you think the picture could represent the term hero.	Put a check if you think the picture could represent the term hero.

During Direct Instruction

Formative assessment must take place throughout the learning process. When teachers continuously and routinely take the temperature of the room, they are gathering invaluable, intangible feedback that immediately informs teaching and keeps the instructional loop alive. Don't underestimate the value in simply listening, circulating throughout the room, questioning, observing body language, confused facials, nodding of heads, or off-task behaviors. These are intuitive indicators of whether your students are understanding your content. However, there are more concrete ways to gather data on the level of understanding your students are obtaining.

Analogies

When teaching new content, consider pausing and asking students to create an analogy between the new materials and something with which they are familiar. While very difficult for the students because of its abstract nature, it will provide insight into how closely your students are conceptualizing the new material.

Freeze Frames

After reading a scene from a fractured fairy tale, allow students to freeze various scenes from the play by becoming the characters. Students must consider poses, facials, body language, etc. to capture a true rendition of the setting and characters involved. In a social studies lesson, students could freeze important scenes from a event in history.

Four Corners

You can incorporate movement into your lesson by playing an academic version of four corners. You may ask students to go to Corner 1 if they strongly support the actions of Stanley Yelnats in *Holes*, Corner 2 if they agree, Corner 3 if they disagree, or Corner 4 if they strongly disagree. They must have a rationale for their decision based on textual evidence. Similarly, you could use Four Corners to review information. After teaching about Ancient Egypt, you could assign students at random to one of four corners to collaborate with new group members: Corner 1 – religion/gods; Corner 2 – Pharoahs and mummies; Corner 3 – architecture/pyramids; Corner 4 – government/social classes. These groups share out, at which point you can address any major points that have been missed and correct any misunderstandings. This is also an excellent option for allowing students to create multiple-choice questions for other groups.

Graffiti Wall

Upper elementary students can collect significant quotes from characters in a book or historical figures by writing them on the wall! Simply take bulletin board paper and hang it on a section of your classroom or hallway walls and allow them to begin splashing their thoughts onto it. In addition, grades K–2 could use a graffiti wall as a space to collect their thoughts and opinions with pictures or single words reactions to a text. Your purpose could vary greatly depending on content and objective, but allowing a space for students to think out loud in a visual manner stimulates other students' thoughts as well as provides an insider's view for the teacher.

Pizza Wheel

We also like to use a "pizza wheel" to review material that students are assigned to read before class. Rather than simply listing information, using the wheel allows students to visually organize their thinking. Each student writes a fact that he or she learned on one of the pizza slices. Then, working in small groups, students pass their papers to the next group member, who also writes a fact. This continues around the circle until each pizza is full. Students can discuss the material, using the pizza wheels as a prompt.

Pizza Wheel

Student: ______________________________

Topic: ______________________________

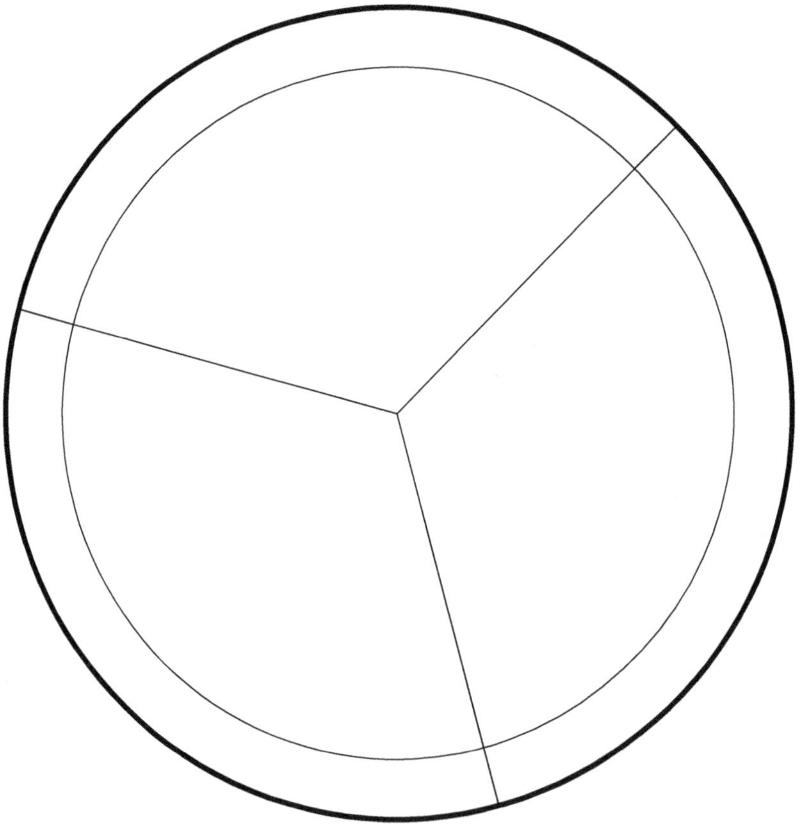

Although you can measure your students' understanding in an oral discussion, asking each student to write his or her response ensures that all students are involved in the lesson and provides an opportunity for every student to respond. The rigor is increased, as each student is required to participate.

One adaptation is Cartwheels, in which each group writes two key points, then passes the information to another group who revises, deletes, or adds to it. This continues until the information has rotated to all groups.

You've Got Mail

In one of their blogs, Edutopia (www.edutopia.org/resource/checking-understanding-download) recommends using You've Got Mail. As the author describes it,

> Each student writes a question about a topic on the front of an envelope; the answer is included inside. Questions are then "mailed" around the room. Each learner writes his or her answer on a slip of scratch paper and confirms its correctness by reading the "official answer" before she places his or her own response in the envelope. After several series of mailings and a class discussion about the subject, the envelopes are deposited in the teacher's letterbox.

After Instruction

Exit Slips

Exit slips are an effective way to receive instant feedback on a student's level of mastery.

There are two functions of exit slips, each of which supports different aspects of your instruction.

Types of Exit Slips

- Demonstrate understanding of content
- Stimulate students' self-awareness
- Focus on instructional strategies

Demonstrate Understanding of Content

Probably the most common use of exit slips is for students to explain what they learned during the lesson. Although you can simply ask them to write down something they learned, you can also extend that to ask for a higher level of understanding. At the most basic level, simply ask the students, "What are your three take aways from today's lesson?" It's quite revealing to read what your students actually heard you say that day. You can quickly address misconceptions or reemphasize missed points the next day.

Stimulate Students' Self-Awareness

In these exit slips, students judge how well they understand the content. For example, you might ask students to rank themselves on a scale of 1–3: 3 – I can teach this to a partner. 2 – I need a little help, but if I talk to someone else I will probably understand this. 1 – I'm lost and need help. Ask students, "How would you rate your understanding of what we discussed in class today?" You might place a laminated poster by your door. On the poster, use a picture of a stoplight, mountain, or another symbol that is relevant to students. Then pose the question. For example, "How comfortable do you feel with using capital letters with proper nouns in your writing?" or "How confident are you in your ability to explain the difference between democracy and monarchy to another student?" Have students write their name on a sticky note and place it on or near the term or picture that matches their comfort level. If you would like students' responses to be confidential, have them write their choice on a notecard and place it in a box near the door.

Self-Assessment		
Mountain	*Stoplight*	*Rocket*
	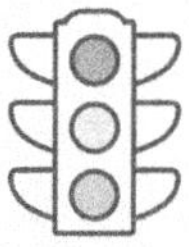	
Base (need some help to get started) Climbing the Mountain (I'm making progress) At the Top (I've learned this and am ready to move on to something else) *Notice this picture symbolizes that the student will have various moments of success and opportunities to learn.	Red (I'm stuck where I am) Yellow (I need some help before I move on) Green (ready to move on)	Purple (on the launchpad – ready to learn) Yellow (firing up the engines – getting started) Green (everything is fine – I'm where I need to be) Blue (soaring – moving beyond to new levels)

Another option is to use A Bump in the Road. With a bump in the road, students reflect on their learning and identify two to four points where they hit bumps in the road, or struggles. Then they partner with another student to see if they can work their way through their struggle.

Focus on Instructional Strategies

When you use an exit slip in this manner, it gives students an opportunity to provide feedback on the effectiveness of specific instructional strategies used to support their learning. This type of exit strategy is best implemented weekly.

> ***Sample Prompts for Exit Slips on Instructional Strategies***
>
> - Did the anchor chart help or hinder your learning during today's lesson? Explain your answer.
> - This week during class, you used an interactive reading guide to help you and your partner process the text. In what ways did this instructional strategy support your learning? In what ways did this instructional strategy hinder your learning?
> - Before we approached the topic for today, we watched a video to provide the background knowledge necessary for understanding the content in our challenging text. To what degree did you find this helpful? How else might we have frontloaded you for the text we read?
> - Today we worked together in small groups to make meaning of the subject matter. How did this facilitate your learning?

No matter what type of exit slip you are using, you'll want to find a way to manage the information. With today's technology, there are a variety of ways to collect exit slip information from your students. With any mobile device, students can access a digital platform and immediately push answers out to the teacher, who then has the ability to display the class's thinking as a whole on the screen or choose a select few to further discuss.

> ***Electronic Exit Slips***
>
> - Google Forms
> - Mentimeter
> - Recap
> - Plickers
> - Twitter
> - Geddit
> - Poll Everywhere
> - ExitTicket
> - Lino
> - Padlet (will soon require a fee)

Do This . . . Not That

Another way to ask students to demonstrate their understanding of a learning strategy is to use Do This . . . Not That. After learning a new strategy, students complete a two-column chart, explaining what you should do when using the strategy, and what you should not do.

	Do This	*Not That*
Reading an Informational Text	First, notice the title and any pictures, charts, or bolded words that may provide information to help you understand the text. Second, read through the text one time, circling words that you do not know. Third, determine if you need to look those words up to understand the text. Fourth, summarize, in your own words, what the text was about.	Read quickly through the text without pausing to question whether or not you understand it.

Utilize Technology Resources

In today's technology-rich society, it's important to incorporate tech-based resources into our formative assessment.

Journaling/Written Conversations

Journaling is a unique way to capture student thinking that allows them to process what they learned. You may consider using journals as responses to literature or for processing writing in a language arts classroom or for writing journals of historical figures or news reports of an international event in social studies. While this formative assessment tool may take longer for the teacher to evaluate, it provides an authentic snapshot of what each student is thinking. In grades 3–5, you may even consider allowing students to blog! The blog is used solely for classroom instructional purposes, but now they have a trendy way to reflect on their learning. As the teacher, you have full access to the blog as well. This spin on journaling uses a modality that fascinates students. You may also allow students to create a vlog, or a video blog if they are particularly tech saavy.

Written conversations are another way to prompt reflection in students. Responding to a question you've posed at the end of a lesson, students would begin to write their thoughts. After a few minutes, they might exchange with a peer, who reads their response, and adds to the reflection. Students can ask/answer clarification questions for one another, discuss the most important points in the lesson, or share ideas for solving a problem, starting a debate. The subject matter and level of question is up to the teacher's discretion. This could also work in a Google Doc, shared between two students and the teacher, or between student and teacher. K–2 students may choose to have verbal conversations in small, teacher-led groups to foster reflection skills.

Screencasting/Educreations

It's also important to assess what is happening with students' use of technology during instruction. Screencasting allows students to record what happens on a particular device screen and add narration to the recording to make a video file. They can take simple screenshots or collect more extensive information. This process allows you to see and hear their learning process, which gives you a deeper understanding of what is happening.

Video and Audio

Another option is to ask students to use either audio or video to record their thinking. Rather than simply seeing the final answer from a student, you are able to understand where they may have made a mistake, which allows you to help them learn at a higher level. FlipGrid and SeeSaw offer various options for recording audio/video student responses.

Other Tools

There are many other tools that allow you to incorporate formative assessment in your classroom. Let's look at a sampling.

Formative Assessment Tools	
Online Platform	*Functions*
Padlet	♦ Acts as digital KWL that can be used to gather student feedback.
Socrative	♦ Develop quizzes, exit tickets, use before or after instruction and organizes data for teacher analysis.
Backchannelchat.com	♦ Pause during a lesson or reading of a text and ask everyone to comment/respond to a question or prompt.
Nearpod.com	♦ Push content out to student devices, one screen at a time, and allow them to interact digitally through multiple choice, open-ended response, annotating text online, drawing on a blank canvas, exploring a virtual 3D image, etc. Provides a way for teachers to facilitate a lesson and get immediate real-time feedback as to what your students are thinking.
EdPuzzle	♦ Use any video from a myriad of online sources and insert pause points where students must gather thoughts, answer a question, make a prediction, etc. before they can continue the video. Completely customize a student-directed video lesson and gather feedback via student responses in real time.
Explaineverything.com	♦ Watch your students' thinking. Explain Everything is an interactive whiteboard that asks students to explain their thinking through a problem or through a prompt. Focus on quality over quantity.

FlipGrid	♦ Use any IOS device to create a video response to a question or prompt. Because you can't have a high-quality conversation with every student every day, this allows you to see what they know via explanation.
Kahoot	♦ Use gaming to review! This assessment platform is game based but allows teachers to create content and disaggregate data.
Go Formative	♦ Upload documents, create your own questions, embed videos or pictures . . . and receive immediate data on student performance.
Educreations	♦ Allows students to draw and/or type their understanding of a concept while recording it in real time with voice explanation of the work they are completing.
SeeSaw	♦ Students can share their learning via video/audio/writing with teachers, classmates, and/or parents.
EduBlog	♦ Blogging online, as a method of reflection and twenty-first-century mode of writing, starting as early as second grade.

Rigorous Summative Assessments

Summative assessments are typically used at the end of a chapter, unit, or topical study to assess students' overall understanding. They also form the basis for grades, particularly those used to compute a final grade for the report card. Although they can be used for diagnostic information, they differ from formative assessments in that their focus is different.

Matching Questions

Matching tests are an easy, quick way to assess a wide range of student knowledge. However, it is difficult to assess at a higher level of rigor, as most matching tests measure basic recall questions. Depending on the items, students can guess rather than truly demonstrate understanding.

What are the best strategies for developing quality matching tests? First, make sure there is one best option for each item you list. Ensure that students can see why the items match so there is clear evidence that students understand the connection. Also, provide more examples than matching items. For example, if you have a list of vocabulary terms and then definitions, add one or two extra definitions to increase the rigor.

Sometimes you need to ask less rigorous questions, but if you use an expanded matching format, in which you create three columns that must be matched, it allows you to increase the rigor. It provides a better opportunity to measure what students know. In this case, you'll also notice there are more choices than items, which requires students to narrow down the answer.

English Headings for Three-Column Matching Test		
Type of Sentence	*Punctuation Used*	*Example*

Social Studies Headings for Three-Column Matching Test		
Event	*Cause*	*Effect*

True–False Tests

True–false tests are an excellent way for students to determine the accuracy of a statement, agree with opinions, and define terms. As with matching items, they are graded quickly and easily, and students can answer a wide range of questions in a short amount of time. However, once again, questions are typically low-level recall questions, and you may not be sure students understand the question or if they are simply guessing. To combat this and to increase the rigor, require students to rewrite any false choices as true statements, which does require them to demonstrate a true understanding of the content. Keep in mind that your questions should also be at a rigorous level rather than requiring rote memorization of knowledge.

Multiple-Choice Tests

Multiple-choice tests are probably the most commonly used tests in classrooms across the nation, and they have several benefits. Although due in part to preparation for standardized tests, they are also easy to score. They also apply to a wide range of cognitive skills, including higher-order-thinking ones. Finally, incorrect answers, if written correctly, can help you diagnose a student's problem areas. Disadvantages include that the questions can't measure a student's ability to create or synthesize information and that students can guess an answer.

There are many ways to write multiple-choice questions that allow you to increase the rigor. First, choose a question that moves beyond basic recall. Next, create choices for the stem that are clearly correct or incorrect without making them too easy. In other words, if we provide examples that are clearly off topic, it makes it easier for students to guess. Although some teachers do not like to use "all of the above," "none of the above," or "a and d" options, we do find they require upper level elementary students to think at a higher level. Remember, you know your students; adapt our suggestions so they match your students' needs.

Short-Answer Questions

Short-answer questions are an expanded form of fill-in-the-blank. Responses are not as long as essays, but they usually include more than one sentence. Because students are required to create a response, they are more rigorous than the types of items we've already discussed. You'll need to build rigor into the context of your questions. Although more challenging to grade than matching, true–false, fill-in-the-blank, and multiple-choice questions, they are easier to assess than essay questions. The two examples are typical of short-answer questions.

English/Language Arts Example

Based on what you have read in *The Lemonade War*, compare and contrast the two siblings' personalities to someone you know in your life.

Social Studies Example

What is the role of a bank in an economy?

Essay Questions

Essay questions are one of the most common assessments used in today's classrooms. Essay questions are extremely effective for measuring complex learning. Opportunities for guessing are removed, so you can truly measure what students understand. There are several disadvantages, including the amount of time to grade them, the subjective nature of grading, and the dependency of the answer on the student's writing ability.

When you are writing essay questions, crafting the question is particularly important. You want to be sure the complexity of the learning outcome is reflected in a clear, focused manner. It's also important to provide explicit instructions as to your expectations.

As with any questions, you can write items at a lower or higher level. In our case, we want to strive for rigorous questions as much as possible. There are times that, with primary students, we do want to give them the opportunity to provide an extended response. In those situations, their responses are typically verbal, although we have seen teachers who use one or more sentence prompts in second grade to allow for an essay-type response.

English/Language Arts Example

We have all faced challenges in our lives and have read about others who have experienced conflict. Using the stories we've read in class, write an essay about a problem one of the characters faced. Explain how the character's choices helped him or her overcome the challenge. Then, describe someone in real life who has faced a similar problem. How have they dealt with the challenge? Conclude by providing a set of recommendations for someone who is facing the challenges you have discussed.

Social Studies Example

People are sometimes forced to move from place to place to survive. Write an essay that explains the various ways nomads benefit from migrating often. Next, describe the problems they experience when moving. Finally, explain how becoming a nomad would affect you in terms of your family, friends, schools, and other interests.

Performance-Based Assessments

Performance-based assessments are a type of summative assessment, but they differ from traditional testing. They are focused on students performing in some manner to demonstrate their understanding. Typically, performance-based assessments are more rigorous because students must go in depth to complete the performance, project, or portfolio. We have discussed projects and project-based and problem-based learning in Chapter 3, which provides some exemplars of performance-based assessments.

Sample Performance-Based Assessments

- Photo Essays
- Performance
- Projects
- Storyboards
- Portfolios

Grading

Grading is one of the most challenging parts of a rigorous classroom. Many of the aspects of grading, such as whether to grade homework, are individual choices for a teacher. No matter your decision, help your parents understand grading. Grading has likely changed since they were in school. As our colleague Abbigail Armstrong explains, on her son's report card, she thought NE meant does not meet expectations, but after talking with the teacher she discovered it means not assessed during this cycle or grading period. She was confused because she was unfamiliar with the terminology and NE was not on the grading key. Let's look at the indicators of effective grading.

> ***Effective GRADING Indicators***
>
> **G**rade according to a policy
> **R**ubrics are helpful
> **A**lign grading to standards
> **D**on't count attendance, effort, or behavior
> **I**nvolve students in grading
> **N**ever give zeroes
> **G**rade for quality, not completion

Grade According to a Policy

In a rigorous classroom, teachers provide a clear grading policy so that students and parents know what to expect. Ideally, you would work together with teachers at your grade level, in your team, or in your department so there is consistency. However, that may not be possible. Grading policies should be communicated early in the school year, ideally in writing. They are also important for all grade levels, including the primary level. Remember to match the language and format of the policy to the level of your students.

> ***Sample Categories for Grading Policy***
>
> - Purpose of grading
> - How grades, progress, and challenges will be communicated
> - How grades are determined (tests, projects, homework, etc.)
> - Percentage of overall grade each item/category counts (project is 30% of grade)
> - Homework (how often you assign it, how it counts, penalties for late work, possibility of redoing work)
> - Late penalties
> - Redo policy
> - Ways to communicate with teacher

Rubrics Are Helpful

Rubrics are written descriptions of the criteria used to grade an assignment. They show students what they are expected to do. We've adapted Todd Stanley's five steps to creating rubrics from his book *Performance-Based Assessment for 21st-Century Skills.*

Steps to Creating a Rubric

1. Decide the range of performance.
2. Create categories.
3. Provide descriptors in each category.
4. Have a tiered system of descriptors.
5. Make sure the descriptors are specific and include an emphasis on quality in addition to or instead of quantity.

Kindergarten English/Language Arts: Storyboard Rubric

Glowing!	*Growing!*	*Needs Watering (redo)*
I pasted all pictures in order so that they tell a story. 	I pasted most pictures in order. 	I need to rearrange my pictures so they tell a story. 
I colored my pictures with colors that create feelings that match the story. 	I colored my pictures. 	I need to work on coloring my pictures. 
I have a clear beginning, middle, and end to my story. 	It may be hard to see a beginning, middle, and end in my story. 	I have not included a clear beginning, middle, and end. 

Grades 2–5 English/Language Arts: Storyboard Rubric		
Glowing!	*Growing!*	*Needs Watering (redo)*
The storyboard ♦ presents a clearly focused story through pictures and text ♦ is organized in sequential order with a clear beginning, middle, and end ♦ includes a main character who experiences a problem, which is resolved by the end of the story	The storyboard ♦ presents a somewhat focused story using mostly pictures or text, but not both ♦ organizes events in order ♦ includes a main character with a problem	The storyboard ♦ is unfocused ♦ lacks organization; details are not in sequential order ♦ does not appear to have a main character

Grades 3–5 Social Studies Project Rubric: Photo "History Telling" Project		
Glowing!	*Growing!*	*Needs Watering (redo)*
The project ♦ clearly "tells" the story of this historical event/time period ♦ includes vivid, well-chosen photos/paintings, charts, graphs, news headings, and other visuals to make the event/time period "come alive" ♦ captures the mood of the event/time period with appropriate background music	The project ♦ attempts to "tell" the story of this historical event/time period, but may not provide a full, accurate depiction ♦ relies primarily on 1–2 types of visuals to tell the story of this event/time period ♦ includes background music that may have a disconnect with mood of the event/time period	The project ♦ is unable to "tell" the story of this historical event/time period ♦ relies primarily on 1–2 types of visuals to tell the story of this event/time period ♦ includes background music that may have a disconnect with mood of the event/time period

Align Grading to Standards

It's important to align your grading to your standards, goals, and objectives. That may sound basic, but I've often seen an assignment that called for certain outcomes based on the standards, but the grade was based on other criteria. How frustrating for a student! For example, I spoke with one teacher who assigned a written extended response to her students. When she graded it, however, the items that were allocated the most points were neatness and spelling. Whether the student actually answered the question and provided evidence for the response were small portions of the grade. This isn't fair to students. You can count those items, but the main focus of your grade should be whether it meets the standards, goals, and objectives.

When Creating Standards-Based Assessments. . .	
Do This. . .	*Not This. . .*
1. Thoroughly read and understand the purpose of the standard. 2. The verb is important, but pay close attention to what comes after the verb; that is usually the true depth of the question or standard. 3. Design an assessment that accurately measures the standards before beginning the unit. This includes determining the format of the assessment.	1. Don't just merely skim the standard. 2. Don't just zoom in on the verb; the noun phrase that follows is important as well. 3. Don't wait to create your assessment at the end of the unit. This is like taking shots at a target and then drawing in the bullseye wherever most of the arrows landed.

Consider the two following rubrics. The first option is what we often see when teachers are trying to penalize students for poor "studenthood" behaviors by assigning a disproportionate number of points to criteria unrelated to knowledge of content or skill (i.e., not following directions, not formatting correctly). Not only that, but it requires minimal thinking and surface-level comprehension. The second rubric requires higher-level thinking skills such as making connections, synthesizing research from various sources, and analyzing information recorded.

History Project #1: Wanted Poster

We have studied Blackbeard, the infamous pirate. You will create a wanted poster that explains what he is wanted for, what his appearance may be, and where he may be found. The information on the poster must include:

1. Poster **MUST** be on an 8 1/2 × 11 sheet of paper. **(10 points)**
2. Mug shot – we need to know what they look like! **(10 points)**
3. First and last name of your historical figure. **(5 points)**
4. Birth date and year of death. **(5 points)**
5. What country were they born in **and** where did they do their work? **(10 points)**
6. What are they famous (wanted) for? Explain in 2–3 complete sentences, in your own words, for full credit. **(30 points)**
7. A fact that you found interesting **OR** a quote by the person. **(10 points)**
8. Print out or photocopy of your sources with info highlighted. **(15 points)**
9. Your name on the bottom right corner. **(5 points)**

Revision of Grading for Wanted Poster	
Percentage of Grade	*Requirements*
20%	Connections: A short narrative includes key life events, family, possible associates, other locations visited, or other places the person lived to help with locating the person.
25%	Synthesis based on using two sources of information. Information in paper is synthesized from both sources rather than summarized from an isolated source. It is also cited appropriately to demonstrate synthesis.
25%	Analysis: As a conclusion, a narrative blurb includes an analysis of the individual strengths/weaknesses and possible warnings for those who approach him! Although your opinion, analysis should be based on the information gathered.
20%	Written Narrative: Overall flow and quality of writing, appropriate information included, extraneous information excluded. Quotes and other information support key points made throughout the paper.
10%	Basic Requirements: Completion of all aspects of assignment, 8 × 10-inch paper, "mug shot," your name at the bottom right corner, reference list on the back, word-processed narrative with 12-point font and 1-inch margins, minimum of 2 sources, and photocopy of sources with information highlighted.

It is critical when creating scoring guides or rubrics for your assignments that expectations are clear and that the point values primarily measure growth in skills and knowledge gained rather than failure to pay attention to every small detail simply to complete the task.

Don't Count Attendance, Effort, or Behavior

One of the mistakes we made as teachers was grading on things that didn't involve the actual work. For example, if a student "tried hard," we gave them credit for their effort. So as long as they attempted to do the work, the student received partial credit, whether or not any of it was correct. We've since learned to give students multiple opportunities to complete the work correctly, along with coaching the student, but effort alone does not equate to a high grade.

Next, we unconsciously graded based on behavior. It wasn't that blatant, of course, but if I had a student who was well behaved and there was a questionable call on the grade, I gave the student the benefit of the doubt. We should have graded equally, no matter what a student's behavior was. But we were inexperienced and didn't realize what we were doing.

Finally, it's easy to incorporate attendance into grading, but that isn't a fair assessment of a student's understanding of content. If a student was absent, we might take points off for each day he or she was late with the assignment. It didn't matter why they were absent; our policies demanded points taken off for late work. In effect, we penalized students because they weren't at school. Some had good reasons for missing, some less so. But the bottom line was that we were choosing to grade not on their work but on their presence.

Now we would remove these three factors from grading. A grade should reflect the quality of work, not anything else.

Involve Students in Grading

Students feel more ownership when they are involved in the grading process. So include them. Be sure they understand what the grade represents, have them look at samples and grade the items themselves, ask them to self-assess their work, and let them create rubrics. In one classroom, the students determined the levels for rubrics.

Student-Created Categories

4. . . . overachiever
3. . . . proficient – got it
2. . . . stuck in the middle
1. . . . at the bottom

As the teacher explained, "I didn't particularly like the names for some of the levels, but the students chose them, so I stayed with them."

After students create the levels, guide them through the process of what would be an "A" or "B," etc. Student ownership doesn't mean you aren't involved; it simply means you guide the process rather than doing it all yourself. After the rubric is finished, ask students to assess a sample paper so they see how the rubric applies to actual work. Then revise it together, and you can move forward with its use. It's an excellent way for students to be invested in grading.

Never Give Zeroes

Too often, students don't complete work that requires a demonstration of learning. Typically, this results in a low grade. We often think this means students learn the importance of responsibility, but more often they learn that if they are willing to "take a lower grade or a zero," then they do not actually have to complete their work. For some, that is a preferable alternative to completing assignments. Perhaps they don't fully understand the task, or they may simply not want to complete it. However, if we truly have high expectations for students, we don't let them off the hook for learning. We discussed options in Chapter 2 in which students are given multiple opportunities to master their learning. This is far more rigorous than allowing students to not learn. Requiring quality work, work that meets the teachers' expectations, lets students know that the priority is learning, not simple completion of an assignment.

Grade for Quality, Not Completion

That said, in addition to holding students accountable for completing tasks, be sure that your grade reflects the quality of the work, not merely completion or the quantity of included items. A rigorous curriculum will assess the depth of thought and analysis in student responses by taking into account quality indicators.

Indicators	
Quality Indicators	*Completion Indicators*
Completed assignment by demonstrating a depth of understanding Included a detailed explanation Chose the best or most effective strategy to answer a research question or short-answer question	Completed assignment Included surface-level explanation Used easiest, quickest strategy to finish work quickly

Conclusion

Assessments are a crucial part of a rigorous classroom. In addition to incorporating regular formative assessment throughout your lessons, you'll want to revise or write summative assessments that move beyond basic questions that allow students to simply guess an answer, rather than demonstrating understanding.

Points to Ponder

- The most important thing learned. . .
- One strategy I want to implement now. . .
- One strategy I want to save for later. . .
- I'd like to learn more about. . .
- I'd like to share with other teachers. . .

7

Collaborating to Improve Rigor

An important part of raising the level of rigor in your classroom and school is collaborating with other teachers. There are various options and purposes for working together. Many teachers are members of professional learning communities (PLCs). The term has become so commonplace that it can mean any type of collaboration. The original meaning of a professional community of learners reflected the commitment of teachers and leaders who continuously seek to grow professionally and act upon their new learning.

Characteristics of PLCs

There are three defining characteristics of PLCs. First, professional learning communities are focused on student learning. As DuFour, DuFour, Eaker, and Many (2006) promote, the goal is to improve student learning by improving what you do in the classroom. Next, there is a culture of collaboration among the participants. You've probably worked in or seen a team of teachers who were assigned to a task; each performed his or her part of the task, and then they walked away. That's not a true PLC. In a PLC, teachers collaborate to move beyond tasks and learn together. Finally, professional learning communities focus on results, no matter what it takes. Although there may be a discussion of challenges, they are not used as excuses.

Benefits of Professional Learning Communities

There are many ways professional learning communities provide advantages for teachers. Opportunities for collaborative inquiry and the learning related to it allow teachers to develop and share their learning. The ultimate benefit of a professional learning community is a positive impact on learning for everyone – including students.

Benefits for Teachers

- Reduced isolation
- Increased commitment to mission and goals of the school
- Collective responsibility for students' success
- Likelihood of professional renewal
- Higher satisfaction, higher morale, lower rates of absenteeism
- Commitment to making significant and lasting changes
- Greater likelihood of undertaking systemic change
- Enhanced learning that defines good teaching and classroom practice
- Creation of new knowledge and beliefs about teaching and learners

Source: Adapted from Hord and Sommers (2008); DuFour and Marzano (2011)

Types of Professional Learning Communities

There are many different types of collaborative teams. Options for collaborative teams can be used to determine which option best fits your needs.

Options for Collaborative Teams	
Option	*Description*
Faculty-wide teams	Participation of the entire faculty in teams focused on the same issue
Interdisciplinary teams	Teams across grade or content areas or that share common planning time or the same students
Grade-level teams	Focus on students at a single grade level
Vertical teams	Working together across grade levels
Subject-area teams	Focus within a single content area
Special-topic teams	Teams formed around topics of interest
Between-school teams	Teachers from more than one school work together

Source: Adapted from: Team to Teach: A Facilitator's Guide to Professional Learning Teams. National Staff Development Council, 2009

Scheduling Time for Professional Learning Communities

Successful professional learning communities provide time for you and other teachers to work together to meet, talk about rigor in your school, and identify strategies for making your classroom more rigorous. Although you may not have control over scheduling in your school, these ideas provide a starting point for a discussion with school and district leadership.

Providing Collaborative Time	
Strategy	*Description*
Common Planning	When teachers share a common planning period, they may use some of the time for collaborative work.
Parallel Scheduling	Special teachers (PE, music, art, etc.) are scheduled so that grade-level or content-area teachers have common planning.
Shared Classes	Teachers in more than one grade or team combine their students into a single large class for specific instruction, and the other teachers can collaborate.
Faculty Meeting	Find other ways to communicate the routine items shared during faculty meetings and reallocate that time to collaborative activities.
Adjust Start or End of Day	Members of a team, grade, or entire school agree to start their workday early or extend their workday one day a week to gain collaborative time.
Late Start or Early Release	Adjust the start or end of the school day for students and use the time for collaborative activity.
Professional Development Days	Rather than traditional large-group professional development, use the time for teams of teachers to engage in collaborative work.

Are You Ready?

Before we discuss options for PLCs, let's take a moment to self-assess your willingness to participate in a professional learning community. A PLC requires a commitment, and it's important that you participate in the process with a full understanding of what you need to do.

Self-Assess Your Willingness to Participate in a PLC	
Willingness to Participate in a PLC	*Yes/No (Why or Why Not)*
I want to use my knowledge and skills to help other teachers.	
I want other teachers to share their knowledge and skills to help me improve my teaching.	
I am willing to participate in and promote open, honest communication.	
I will participate in a collaboration that is focused on improving student learning, building shared knowledge about best practice, and making a difference in terms of results, no matter what.	
I will honor my commitments to members of my PLC.	
I want to analyze student work at a higher level, set goals based on that data, and implement effective teaching practices to meet those goals.	
I am willing to try and adapt new instructional practices, even if they are not successful the first time.	
I will help establish team goals, norms, and protocols to ensure collaborative work and participate in adjustments needed to ensure this focus.	

Activities for Professional Learning Communities

Let's turn our attention to the types of activities PLCs can use to impact student learning. We'll look at five options.

Five Types of Activities

1. Learning walks
2. Lesson studies
3. Charette
4. Technology-based options
5. Discussions

Learning Walks

Although we sometimes think that learning walks are for administrators, we are recommending that teachers participate in learning walks. They are not evaluative; rather, they are designed to help teachers learn from each other. Additionally, the goal is to identify areas of instructional strengths as well as possible challenges. You may also want to begin by looking only for positive examples in order to build trust.

A school in Chicago organized "I Spy" days. Teachers dropped in on classrooms for 5 to 10 minutes in order to identify positive examples of instruction. Teachers came back together after school with their "detective notebooks" to share what they had seen. It was an invigorating experience for teachers, who said this was the first time they had had a chance to look at other classrooms. As one teacher explained, "I don't get time to visit other teachers' classes. I learned so much, and I have two new ideas I want to implement tomorrow."

Learning Walk Guidelines

1. Work together to identify the purpose of the learning walk.
2. Determine the process, including length of classroom visits as well as what will occur during the visits. Develop and use a consistent tool for participants to use to record their observations and collect data.
3. Inform everyone when the learning walks will occur.
4. Conduct a pre-walk orientation for those participating.
5. Conduct the learning walk and spend no more than 5 minutes in each classroom. Depending on the lesson, talk with the teacher and students, look at student work, and examine the organization of the classroom.
6. Immediately after the walk, ask participants to meet and talk about the information they gathered and how to share it with the faculty. They may develop questions that they would ask to learn more about what is occurring.
7. Develop a plan for sharing the information and for using it to guide your continued school-improvement work.

Lesson Studies

A more formal option than simply working together to craft a lesson, lesson studies emphasize working in small groups to plan, teach, observe, and critique a lesson. It's an excellent refection of the principles of professional learning communities, as the goal is to systematically examine your teaching in order to become more effective.

In a lesson study, teachers work together to develop a detailed plan for a lesson. One member of the group teaches the lesson to his or her students while other members of the group observe. Next, the group discusses their observations about the lesson and student learning.

Teachers revise the lesson based on their observations, then a second group member teaches the lesson, with other members once again observing. Then the group meets to discuss the revised lesson. Finally, teachers talk about what the study lesson taught them and how they can apply the learning in their own classroom.

Cycle for Lesson Studies

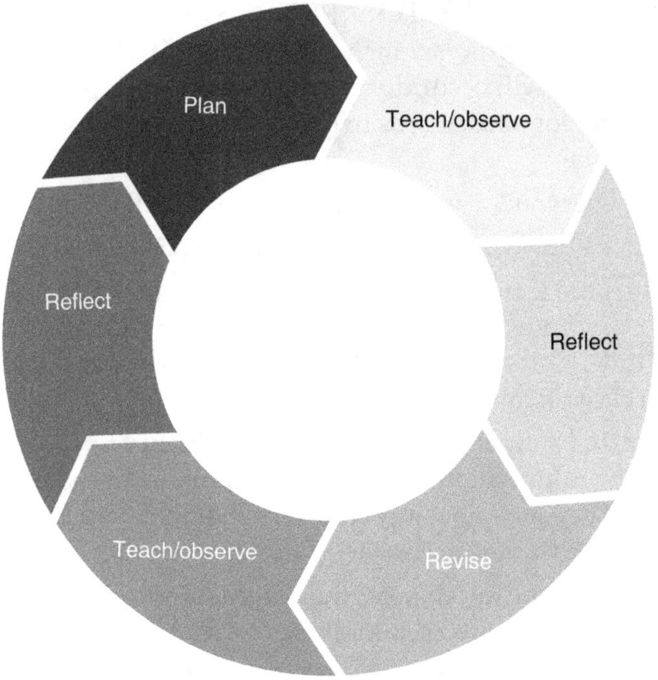

Charrette

A "charrette" is a set of agreed-upon guidelines for talking with colleagues about an issue. The conversation tends to be more trusting and more substantive because everyone knows the guidelines in advance. Charrettes are often used to improve the work while the work is in progress and are not to be used as an evaluative tool. You may be wondering how this differs from a general discussion of an issue. A charrette is typically used when there is a specific issue a teacher needs to address, which at times may have the potential for dissension and therefore needs a more structured approach to the conversation. Additional information about the charrette is available at http://schoolreforminitiative.org/doc/charrette.pdf.

Charrette Protocol

1. A group or an individual from the group requests a charrette when they want others to help them resolve an issue. Often they are at a "sticking point," and the conversation will help them move forward.
2. Another small group is invited to look at the work and a facilitator is used to moderate the discussion.
3. The requesting group or individual presents its work and states what they need or want from the discussion. The conversation is focused by this presentation.
4. The invited group discusses the issue, and the requesting group listens and takes notes. The emphasis is on improving the work, which now belongs to the entire group. "We're in this together" characterizes the discussion.
5. Once the requesting group gets what it needs, it stops the process, summarizes what was learned, thanks participants, and returns to their work.

Source: Adapted from: "Charrette Protocol," written by Kathy Juarez and available on the *School Reform Initiative* website (http://schoolreforminitiative.org/doc/charrette.pdf)

Technology-Based Options

There are a variety of ways that teachers are using technology to enhance their PLCs.

Many teachers use Google Docs to share work samples and lesson plans and wikis to share collaborative work. Others use videos to enhance their opportunities to observe and discuss teaching strategies. Sites such as the Teaching Channel provide informational videos but also provide classroom demonstrations. These allow you to watch and critique teaching without visiting an actual classroom.

Sample Sites for Teaching Videos   **Teaching Channel** (www.teachingchannel.org)   **Engage NY** (www.engageny.org/video-library)   **America Achieves** (http://commoncore.americaachieves.org)   **Teachers Network** (www.teachersnetwork.org/videos/)   **Inside Mathematics** (www.insidemathematics.org/classroom-videos)   **WatchKnowLearn** (www.watchknowlearn.org)   **The 100 Best Video Sites for Teachers** (www.edudemic.com/best-video-sites-for-teachers/)

With the popularity of social media sites, many districts take advantage of that interest. One strategy is to use Twitter chats. Chatham County, North Carolina, sets a regular time for chats, and they invite experts in the designated focus area to participate. This allows teachers to interact and ask more questions than in the traditional model of training.

Monique Flickinger, director of instructional technology of Poudre Schools in Colorado, shares how her district uses Facebook.

> We created a Facebook account, TeachTechPSD, where we post weekly updates on new technology, pictures of classes using tech and other fun things we are learning about. When teachers come to training with us, we ask them to "like" us so that, when they check their own accounts, they will quickly see what we are up to.

Discussions

Collaborative discussions are at the heart of a professional learning community. Oftentimes, we think that we can simply "get together and talk." However, we have all participated in group discussions that were derailed by off-topic discussions, meetings that devolved into complaint sessions, or times when the discussion was fragmented and the goals of the group were not met.

It Begins With Norms

A crucial part of any effective meeting is having a set of meeting standards or operational norms. This includes basic decisions such as the seating arrangements. If you want an open discussion, try to arrange for participants to face each other, perhaps around a table or in a semicircle rather than in rows. Set firm start and end times and stick to them. This shows that you respect the participants' time. If the meeting is lengthy, plan for a break, but again, set a time and adhere to that. Be sure that any speaker knows his or her allocated time and stays within those parameters.

Ask yourself, "How will we maintain our group memory of discussion and decisions?" Do you want to use charts posted visibly in the room, or will you have someone record notes? In today's age of technology, how can you utilize the equipment you have to support the process? You might even consider recording the meeting. A public recording provides visual clues, develops shared ownership, minimizes repetition, reduces status differences among participants, and makes accountability easier.

What are the guidelines for discussion? We often use a "parking lot," which is simply a poster in the room. Participants are given sticky notes, and if there is a question or discussion item that is off the topic, they write it on a note and post it in the parking lot. You can revisit those items at the end of the meeting if there is time, or you can discuss them individually or at another time.

It's also important for everyone to model collaborative discussion. Allowing adequate wait time in response to questions, asking open-ended questions, and giving everyone a chance to speak are the foundational elements of a collaborative discussion. Garmston and Wellman (2013) describe seven norms of collaboration that are helpful as you facilitate discussions.

Seven Norms of Collaboration

1. **Pausing:** Pausing before responding or asking a question allows time for thinking and enhances dialogue, discussion, and decision making.
2. **Paraphrasing:** Using a paraphrase starter that is comfortable for you, such as "As you are . . ." or "You're thinking. . . ," and following the starter with a paraphrase assists members of the group to hear and understand each other as they formulate decisions.
3. **Probing:** Using gentle open-ended probes or inquiries such as, "Please say more . . ." or "I'm curious about . . ." or "I'd like to hear more about . . ." or "Then, are you saying. . . ?" increases the clarity and precision of the group's thinking.
4. **Putting ideas on the table:** Ideas are the heart of a meaningful dialogue. Label the intention of your comments. For example, you might say, "Here is one idea . . ." or "One thought I have is . . ." or "Here is a possible approach . . ."
5. **Paying attention to self and others:** Meaningful dialogue is facilitated when each group member is conscious of self and of others and is aware of not only what he or she is saying but also how it is said and how others are responding. This includes paying attention to learning style when planning for, facilitating, and participating in group meetings.
6. **Presuming positive intentions:** Assuming that others' intentions are positive promotes and facilitates meaningful dialogue and eliminates unintentional put-downs. Using positive intentions in your speech is one manifestation of this norm.
7. **Pursuing a balance between advocacy and inquiry:** Pursuing and maintaining a balance between advocating a position and inquiring about one's own and others' positions assists the group to become a learning organization.

Source: Garmston and Wellman (2013)

Types of Discussions

As we said before, the bulk of time in a professional learning community is spent simply discussing topics and issues. That's why we looked at norms that will help you have effective discussions. Now we'll turn our attention to the types of discussions that typically occur. We've found that most discussions fit in three categories.

Discussion Categories
♦ Focus on instruction ♦ Focus on assessment ♦ Focus on student results

Focus on Instruction

First, discussions can focus on instruction. It is important to determine a more focused topic rather than just generally discuss the broad issue of instruction. Within instruction, you may emphasize standards and their relationship to instruction, instructional strategies, relating assessment to instruction or differentiating instruction with the goal of making any needed adjustments that will increase student learning. These areas are not in any particular order; choose the area that meets your needs and that makes the most sense.

Ideas for Discussion	
Focus Area	*Ideas for Discussion*
Standards	Analyze standards to determine exactly what they mean. Determine if current instruction addresses standards on a surface level or a deeper level. Determine how standards relate to prior year and upcoming year. Determine if particular standards need more or less emphasis. Determine any sequence issues. Determine if there are any particular strategies or assessments that would be particularly effective with certain standards.

continued

Strategies	Analyze current instruction to determine if it is rigorous and if it leads to student growth (perhaps through a review of lesson plans or learning walks). Assess whether instructional strategies are effective, or if there are other strategies that would be more effective. Research and share any new instructional strategies. Determine whether specific instructional strategies are effective for particular groups of students, such as English learners. Research instructional strategies that are effective for particular groups of students, such as English learners (link to differentiation discussions).
Assessment	Analyze how or if current assessments measure all aspects of instruction, including matching the standard. Determine if there are ways to hone assessments to better match standards or instruction. Research and share any new assessment ideas. Assess the rigor of current assessments. Determine if there are areas of instruction and assessment that either do or do not prepare students for any standardized testing. **For all assessments, consider both formative and summative.
Differentiation	Analyze current instruction and assessment (possibly through lesson plans and written tasks) for differentiation. Determine if there are specific groups of students (such as students with special needs or gifted learners) that need differentiation. Research and share differentiation strategies. Develop differentiation strategies and activities to implement in lessons.

***Discussions should always lead to appropriate adjustments to impact student learning.*

Focus on Assessment

Next, discussions may also revolve around assessment. Oftentimes, you will combine the discussion to address instruction and assessment, such as in the topics we listed in the previous section. However, there are times you will want to specifically focus on the quality of the assessments themselves. Ideally, you will compare the assessments to an outside benchmark of quality, including the level of rigor.

An effective discussion can surround the concept of measuring the level of rigor of specific tasks, projects, tests, and other assessments.

Process One for Assessing Tasks, Projects, Tests, and Assessments

1. Review and discuss characteristics of rigorous work during one meeting. You may want to review the samples provided in Chapter 3.
2. Before the next meeting, teachers choose one sample assessment, reflect on the rigor individually and make any desired adjustments.
3. At the second meeting, teachers distribute copies of their sample assessment. Members of the group compare the assignment to the criteria, discuss, and come to a consensus as to whether it is rigorous, and suggest any possible changes.
4. Repeat as often as desired.

Another option is to focus on common assessments. In that case, follow the same process, but skip Step 2.

Our preference is to use Webb's Depth of Knowledge as a set of criteria for comparison.

Partial Characteristics of Rigorous Work Based on Webb's Depth of Knowledge	
Math	*Science*
Requires reasoning, planning, or use of evidence to solve a problem or algorithm. May involve an activity with more than one possible answer. Requires conjecture or restructuring of problems. Involves drawing conclusions from observations, citing evidence, and developing logical arguments for concepts. Uses concepts to solve nonroutine problems.	Requires students to solve problems with more than one possible answer and justify responses. Involves aspects of authentic experimental design processes. Requires drawing conclusions from observations, citing evidence, and developing logical arguments for concepts. Involves using concepts to solve nonroutine problems.

Source: Webbalign.org

We've provided you a full sample of all levels of the criteria for each content in Chapter 3. Remember that Levels 3 and 4 are considered rigorous.

Focus on Student Data

When we say "student data," we typically think of test scores. It is certainly important to review students' scores on summative assessments as well as standardized tests. When we do, we can learn about students' strengths and weaknesses, how well they understand content compared to other students, and how prepared they are for upcoming lessons. However, we can also learn by looking at work students have completed, whether it is formative or summative work. When you examine and evaluate student work, you can clarify your own standards for work, strengthen common expectations for students or align curriculum across classrooms.

Work Samples to Assess Student Data		
Individual Work Sample	*Group Work Samples*	*Multiple Samples for Different Purposes*
Identify student's strengths. Identify student's weaknesses. Identify growth points. Identify needed steps for improvement. Consider what might have caused this level of work (positive or negative). Are there any changes needed in the teacher's instruction to support this student?	Focus on patterns. Identify strengths and weaknesses of the majority of students. Identify any areas of growth by the group. Is any reteaching needed? Are students ready to move to the next level of learning?	Compare samples from different assessments to look for common patterns. Compare samples from different teachers to determine if a similar level of work occurs in different classes. Compare samples from different teachers to determine if a similar level of work received similar grades. Compare samples from different grade levels to ensure appropriate vertical alignment.

It's important that the discussion is focused on results, not on personalities. At the beginning of the process, agree on a process for the discussion.

Looking at Student Work Protocol

- Talk together about the process and how to ensure it is not evaluative.
- Identify ways to gather relevant contextual information (e.g., copy of assignment, scoring guide or rubric).
- Remove student names and any identifying information.
- Select a protocol or guideline for the conversation that promotes discussion and interaction.
- Agree on how to select work samples.
- Establish a system for providing and receiving feedback that is constructive.

Although there are a variety of guides to use during your discussion, we've provided one for you to consider. Other resources are available at www.lasw.org.

Sample Discussion Guide

- How well do students demonstrate understanding of the standard?
- Is it surface-level understanding or a deeper level?
- Did students complete the work at a satisfactory level? What do we consider satisfactory?
- Are there any particular misconceptions you observe?
- Do students show an understanding of prerequisite knowledge?
- What percentage of students are successful? What do we need to do to help the other students?
- What aspects of the assignment did most students master?
- Which parts did most students not master?
- What does the work of the students tell me about the assignment?
- Is there anything I need to adjust for future assignments?

Assess Your Current Efforts

As we finish our discussion, take time to assess the current status of your professional learning communities. It can be used as a self-assessment or used within your PLC. Once you have completed the assessment, share the results and use them to have a conversation about how to strengthen your work in this area.

Assess Your Professional Learning Community		
Rate Your Professional Learning Community Using This Scale:		
1 – Strongly Disagree 2 – Disagree	3 – Neutral 4 – Agree	5 – Strongly Agree
Rating		
1. We're organized into collaborative teams to work on curricular and instructional issues.		
2. Collaboration is embedded into our routine practice.		
3. We have agreed-upon indicators or data points that we will use to measure our progress.		

4. We analyze student achievement data to help us establish goals for our work.	
5. We monitor the learning of each student so that we can monitor and adjust our work.	
6. We maintain a "laser light" focus on results.	
7. Each team member is clear about our goals, student expectations and common assessments.	
8. We use the results of our assessments to identify students who need additional time or support and establish processes to assure that they get the support they need.	
9. We agree to and honor our commitments to members of our collaborative teams.	
10. Our collaboration is focused first on improving student learning.	
11. Our collaboration is also focused on teachers helping others improve.	
12. Our collaborative teams help us build shared knowledge about best practice.	
13. Our teams have established norms and protocols.	
14. Our teams maintain a focus on team goals.	
15. Our collaborative work is monitored and supported.	

Conclusion

If we want to improve our teaching and increase student learning, we will make more progress if we work together. Professional learning communities, when implemented effectively, allow teachers opportunities to participate in activities and discussions focused on improvement.

Points to Ponder

- The most important thing learned. . .
- One strategy I want to implement now. . .
- One strategy I want to save for later. . .
- I'd like to learn more about. . .
- I'd like to share with other teachers. . .

Bibliography

54 Different examples of formative assessment. (n.d.). Retrieved from http://cmrweb.gfps.k12.mt.us/uploads/2/7/3/6/27366965/formative_assessment_ppt.pdf

The Academy of Inquiry Based Learning. (n.d.). *Supporting instructors, empowering students, transforming mathematics learning*. Retrieved from www.inquirybasedlearning.org

Ames, R., & Ames, C. (1990). Motivation and effective teaching. In B. F. Jones & L. Idol (Eds.), *Dimensions of thinking and cognitive instruction*. Hillsdale, NJ: Erlbaum.

Barrell, J. (2007). *Problem-based learning: An inquiry approach* (2nd ed.). Thousand Oaks, CA: Corwin Press.

Benjamin, A. (2008). *Formative assessment for English language arts*. New York, NY: Routledge.

Black, P., Harrison, C., Lee, C., Marshall, B., & William, D. (2004). Working inside the black box: Assessment for learning in the classroom. *Phi Delta Kappan*, *86*, 9–21.

Blackburn, B. R. (2008). Literacy from A to Z: *Engaging students in reading, writing, speaking, & listening*. New York, NY: Routledge.

Blackburn, B. R. (2012). *Rigor made easy*. New York, NY: Routledge.

Blackburn, B. R. (2014). *Rigor in your classroom: A toolkit for teachers*. New York, NY: Routledge.

Blackburn, B. R. (2016a). *Classroom instruction from A to Z: How to promote student learning* (2nd ed.). New York, NY: Routledge.

Blackburn, B. R. (2016b). *Motivating struggling learners: Ten strategies for student success*. New York, NY: Routledge.

Blackburn, B. R. (2017). *Rigor and assessment in the classroom*. New York, NY: Routledge.

Blackburn, B. R. (2018). *Rigor is not a four-letter word* (3rd ed.). New York, NY: Routledge.

Blackburn, B. R. (2019). *Rigor and differentiation in the classroom*. New York, NY: Routledge.

Blackburn, B. R., Armstrong, A., & Miles, M. (2018). Using writing to spark learning in math, science, and social studies. *ASCD Express*, *13*(16). Retrieved from www.ascd.org/ascd-express/vol13/1316-blackburn.aspx?utm_source=ascdexpress&utm_medium=email&utm_campaign=Express%2D13%2D16

Blackburn, B. R., & Witzel, B. (2013). *Rigor for students with special needs.* New York, NY: Routledge.

Blackburn, B. R., & Witzel, B. (2018). *Rigor in the RTI/MTSS classroom.* New York, NY: Routledge.

Class Tech Tips. (n.d.). About Monica – Class tech tips. *Class Tech Tips.* Retrieved July 20, 2018, from https://classtechtips.com/about-monica/

Cleary, J. A., Morgan, T. A., & Marzano, R. J. (2018). *Classroom techniques for creating conditions for rigorous instruction.* West Palm Beach, FL: Learning Sciences International.

CollegeBoard. (2014). *Research foundations: Empirical foundations for college and career readiness.* Retrieved from https://collegereadiness.collegeboard.org/pdf/research-foundations-college-career-readiness.pdf

Curwin, R. L. (2010). *Meeting students where they live: Motivation in urban schools.* Alexandria, VA: Association of Supervision and Curriculum Development.

The DBQ Project. (2018, July 19). The DBQ Project. *The DBQ Project.* Retrieved July 20, 2018, from www.dbqproject.com/

Dr. Karin Hess. (n.d.). Dr. Karin Hess | Cognitive rigor and DoK.

Dr. Karin Hess. Retrieved July 20, 2018, from www.karin-hess.com/cognitive-rigor-and-dok

DuFour, R., DuFour, R., Eaker, R., & Many, T. (2006). *Learning by doing: A handbook for professional learning communities at work.* Bloomington, IN: Solution Tree Press.

DuFour, R., DuFour, R., Eaker, R., & Many, T. (2010). *Learning by doing: A handbook for professional learning communities at work* (2nd ed.). Bloomington, IN: Solution Tree Press.

DuFour, R., DuFour, R., Eaker, R., Many, T. W., & Mattos, M. (2016). *Learning by doing: A handbook for professional learning communities at work* (3rd ed.). Bloomington, IN: Solution Tree Press.

DuFour, R., & Marzano, R. (2011). *Leaders of learning: How district, school, and classroom leaders improve student achievement.* Bloomington, IN: Solution Tree Press.

Engagetheirminds. (2013). *Augmented reality resource page.* Engage Their Minds. Retrieved June 16, 2019, from https://engagetheirminds.com/2013/10/21/augmented-reality-resource-page/

Eubank, T. (2011). *SREB: Instant credit recovery or instant "content" recovery for middle grades: ICR Summary and implementation strategies.* (Unpublished white paper). Retrieved January 3, 2011.

Ferriter, W. M., & Garry, A. (2010). *Teaching the iGeneration: 5 easy ways to introduce essential skills with web 2.0 tools.* Bloomington, IN: Solution Tree Press.

Fielding, L., & Roller, C. (1992, May). Making difficult books accessible and easy books acceptable. *The Reading Teacher*, 678–685.

Fisher, D., & Frey, N. (n.d.). *Scaffolds for learning: The key to guided instruction*. Retrieved June 20, 2017, from www.ascd.org/publications/books/111017/chapters/Scaffolds-for-Learning@-The-Key-to-Guided-Instruction.aspx

Fisher, D., & Frey, N. (2012). *Close reading in elementary schools*. Newark, DE: International Reading Association. Retrieved June 12, 2019, from https://s3-us-west-1.amazonaws.com/fisher-and-frey/documents/Close_Reading_Elem.pdf?mtime=20160813133938

Fisher, D., Frey, N., & Lapp, D. (2012). *Text complexity: Raising rigor in reading*. Newark, DE: International Reading Association.

Garmston, R., & Wellman, B. (2013). *The adaptive school: A sourcebook for developing collaborative groups* (2nd ed.). Norwood, MA: Christopher-Gordon.

Gibson, S. (2013). *Effective framework for primary-grade guided writing instruction*. Reading Rockets. Retrieved July 20, 2019, from www.readingrockets.org/article/effective-framework-primary-grade-guided-writing-instruction

Guskey, T. R., & Bailey, J. M. (2001). *Developing grading and reporting systems for student learning*. Thousand Oaks, CA: Corwin Press.

Hattie, J., & Yates, G. (2008). *Visible learning: A synthesis of over 800 meta-analyses relating to achievement*. New York, NY: Routledge Taylor & Francis Group.

Hattie, J., & Yates, G. (2014). *Visible learning and the science of how we learn*. New York, NY: Routledge Taylor & Francis Group.

Hord, S., & Sommers, W. (2008). *Leading professional learning communities*. Thousand Oaks, CA: Corwin Press.

Iksan, Z. H., & Daniel, E. (2016). Types of wait time during verbal questioning in the science classroom. *International Research in Higher Education, 1*(1), 72–80. Retrieved from http://dx.doi.org/10.5430/irhe.v1n1p72

James, J. G., & Aschner, M. J. (1963). A preliminary report: Analysis of classroom interaction. *Merrill-Palmer Quarterly of Behavior and Development, 9*, 183–194.

Juliani, A. J. (2015). *Inquiry and innovation in the classroom: Using 20% time, genius hour, and PBL to drive student success*. New York, NY: Routledge.

Krebs, D. (2016). *Genius hour in the primary classroom: The genius hour guidebook*. Retrieved July 22, 2019, from www.geniushourguide.org/genius-hour-in-the-primary-classroom/

Lalley, J. P., & Miller, R. H. (2006). Effects of pre-teaching and re-teaching on math achievement and academic self-concept of students with low achievement in math. *Education, 126*(4), 747–755.
Lapp, D. (2016). *Turning the page on complex texts: Differentiated scaffolds for close reading instruction*. Bloomington, IN: Solution Tree Press.
Maiers, A., & Sandvold, A. (2011). *The passion-driven classroom: A framework for teaching and learning*. New York, NY: Routledge.
Marzano, R. J. (2007). *The art of science and teaching: A comprehensive framework for effective instruction*. Alexandria, VA: Association for Supervision and Curriculum Development.
Marzano, R. J. (2010). Giving students meaningful work. *Educational Leadership, 68*, 82–84.
Marzano, R. J. (2012). Art and science of teaching: The many uses of exit slips. *Educational Leadership, 70*(2), 80–81.
Marzano, R. J., Pickering, D. J., & Pollock, J. E. (2001). *Classroom instruction that works: Research-based strategies for increasing student achievement*. Alexandria, VA: Association for Supervision and Curriculum Development.
McTighe, J., & Wiggins, G. (2013). *Essential questions: Opening doors to student understanding*. Alexandria, VA: Association for Supervision and Curriculum Development.
Morgan, N., & Saxton, J. (2006). *Asking better questions* (2nd ed.). Ontario, Canada: Pembroke Publishers.
National Association of Colleges and Employers. (2017). *Career readiness defined*. Retrieved from www.naceweb.org/career-readiness/competencies/career-readiness-defined/
NGSS. (n.d.). *Conceptual shifts in the next generation science standards*. Retrieved August 1, 2017, from www.nextgenscience.org/sites/default/files/Appendix%20A%20-%204.11.13%20Conceptual%20Shifts%20in%20the%20Next%20Generation%20Science%20Standards.pdf
O'Conner, K. (2002). *How to grade for learning: Linking grades to standards*. Thousand Oaks, CA: Corwin Press.
Olge, D. (1986). K-W-L: A teaching model that develops active reading of expository text. *Reading Teacher, 39*, 564–571.
Perkins, D. (2018, January 4). Main. *TeachThought*. Retrieved July 20, 2019, from www.teachthought.com/
Pew Research Center. (2017). Retrieved from www.pewresearch.org/fact-tank/2017/02/15/u-s-students-internationally-math-science/
Pimentel, S. (2013). *College and career readiness standards for adult education*. Retrieved July 20, 2018, from https://lincs.ed.gov/publications/pdf/CCRStandardsAdultEd.pdf

Pitler, H., Hubbell, E. R., & Kuhn, M. (2012). *Using technology with classroom instruction that works* (2nd ed.). Alexandria, VA: Association for Supervision and Curriculum Development.

Popham, W. J. (2008). *Transformative assessment*. Alexandria, VA: Association for Supervision and Curriculum Development.

Regier, N. (2012). Book two: Formative assessment strategies. *Regier Educational Resources*. Retrieved May 21, 2018, from www.stma.k12.mn.us/documents/DW/Q_Comp/FormativeAssessStrategies.pdf

Richardson, W. (2010). *Blogs, wikis, podcasts, and other powerful web tools for classrooms* (3rd ed.). Thousand Oaks, CA: Corwin Press.

Rothstein, D., & Santana, L. (2011). *Make just one change: Teach students to ask their own questions*. Cambridge, MA: Harvard Education Press.

Sample Exit Tickets. (n.d.). Retrieved from http://science-class.net/Assessment/Exit-tickets/exit_tickets.htm

Santa, C., Havens, L., & Macumber, E. (1996). *Creating independence through student-owned strategies*. Dubuque, IA: Kendall/Hunt.

Schlechty, P. (2011). *Engaging students: The next level of working on the work*. San Francisco, CA: Jossey-Bass.

Senn, D., & Marzano, R. (2015). *Engaging in cognitively complex tasks*. West Palm Beach, FL: Learning Sciences International.

Sienkiewicz, E. *What does a performance assessment look like? Here are six examples. Cce.org*. Retrieved July 22, 2019, from https://cce.org/thought-leadership/blog/post/performance-assessment-six-examples

Small, M. (2010). *Good questions: Great ways to differentiate mathematics instruction*. New York, NY: Teachers College Press.

Smith, G. E., & Throne, S. (2010). *Differentiating instruction with technology in K-5 classrooms*. Eugene, OR: International Society for Technology Integration.

Tovani, C. (2011). *So what do they really know? Assessment that informs teaching and learning*. Portland, ME: Stenhouse.

Wiggins, G., & McTighe, J. (2005). *Understanding by design, expanded* (2nd ed.). Alexandria, VA: Association for Supervision and Curriculum Development.

Williamson, G. L. (2006). *Aligning the journey with a destination: A model for K – 16 reading standards*. Durham, NC: MetaMetrics, Inc.

Williamson, R. (2012). *Research into practice: Importance of high expectations*. Oregon Gear Up. Retrieved July 12, 2018, from https://oregongearup.org/sites/oregongearup.org/files/research-briefs/highexpectations.pdf

Williamson, R., & Blackburn, B. R. (2010). *Rigorous schools and classrooms: Leading the way*. New York, NY: Routledge.

Williamson, R., & Blackburn, B. R. (2017). *Rigor in your school: A toolkit for leaders* (2nd ed.). New York, NY: Routledge.
Wyatt, J., Wiley, A., Camara, W., & Proestler, N. (2011). *The development of an index of academic rigor for college readiness*. Washington, DC: The College Board.

www.ingramcontent.com/pod-product-compliance
Lightning Source LLC
Chambersburg PA
CBHW081420230426
43668CB00016B/2299
* 9 7 8 1 1 3 8 5 9 8 9 5 9 *